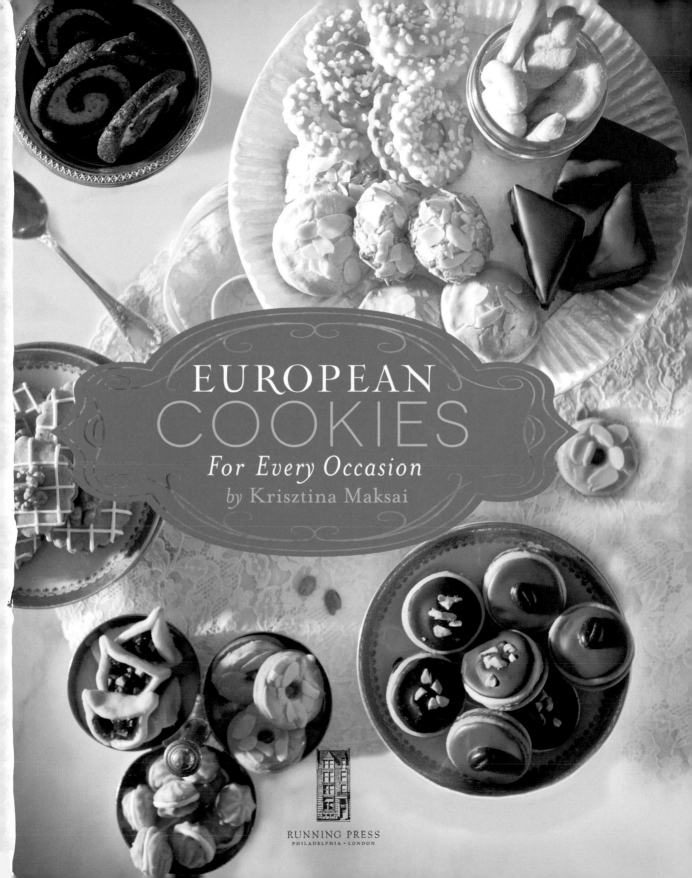

EUROPEAN COOKIES

For Every Occasion

by Krisztina Maksai

RUNNING PRESS
PHILADELPHIA · LONDON

Published by Running Press,
A Member of the Perseus Books Group

Printed in China

Books published by Running Press are available at special discounts for bulk purchases
in the United States by corporations, institutions, and other organizations. For more
information, please contact the Special Markets Department at the Perseus Books Group,
2300 Chestnut Street, Suite 200, Philadelphia, PA 19103, or call (800) 810-4145, ext. 5000,
or e-mail special.markets@perseusbooks.com.

ISBN 978-0-7624-4529-5

Library of Congress Control Number: 2013937227

E-book ISBN 978-0-7624-5070-1

9   8   7   6   5   4   3   2   1

Digit on the right indicates the number of this printing

Edited by Geoffrey Stone
Typography: Allura, Berkeley Book, and Novcento

Running Press Book Publishers
2300 Chestnut Street
Philadelphia, PA 19103-4371

Visit us on the web!
www.runningpress.com
www.offthemenublog.com

To you,
the dear reader,
whoever you might be,
I wrote this for you.

Contents

~ Introduction ~

E ver since I could remember, I have had a sweet tooth. Although I was born in Romania, my family moved to Germany when I was three years old. My first memories of sweets are of street fairs and typical small-town baking sales in Germany. The cakes and cookies mesmerized me. I felt trapped in a spell of their sugarcoated sweetness. We moved often when I was growing up, and living in different countries broadened my horizons.

When I was eleven, I baked my first cake for Easter. It was an apricot-mascarpone German mole cake. From that point on, I fell in love with creating delicious cakes and desserts. Any opportunity I have to bake, I take it. If someone's birthday or a holiday is coming up, the first thing I do is surround myself with books and magazines on baking. I spend hours looking at the pictures and reading recipes to get ideas for creating the best desserts for the occasion.

By the time I turned seven, my family had moved to Hungary, exposing me to another interesting culture. All the countries where I lived and visited had one thing in common: cookies for Christmas. While their form and tastes vary from country to country, they all are delicious and beautiful treats. The possibilities seem endless: filled or topped, sprinkled or glazed, decorated with chocolate or with fruit. That is why my biggest passion is cookies. One Christmas season several years ago, I stepped into the world of delicious small pastries of different shapes and fillings and the most incredible flavors. A few cookie recipes caught my eye, so I decided to bake them. So fragile and small, they were cookies you could eat in just one bite. While that baking experience was not an immediate success, I had so much fun doing it. The decorations were so precise, I was essentially painting each cookie, and my family reacted as though I had offered them pieces of edible art.

Since then, I have baked many different kinds of cookies for Christmas. Now, when my name comes up among family members or close friends, it always makes them think of the cookies and cakes that I bake. After a while each Christmas I would try to break my own record. How many different kinds of cookies could I bake? Two years ago, I broke my personal record by baking twenty-seven different types of cookies. I worked on the cookies for two or three weeks. I baked at night as a relaxing way to pass the time, but the only downside was all the dirty dishes! Fortunately, I have an incredibly caring and sweet grandmother. She would chase me away from the sink filled with mountains of unwashed dishes, saying, "Leave it up to me, I am a professional!" I gave her a smooch on the cheek and went happily back to making cookies.

I realized very quickly that baking is like learning how to drive or learning a new language. With practice, you will improve. I believe that anybody can do it with an accurate recipe, precise instructions, and a few baking tips. Of course, in the beginning the result may not be perfect, but don't give up. Everybody made mistakes at the beginning, even the professional confectioners. It will get easier. You will learn from your mistakes, and eventually you will become confident enough to alter recipes to your own tastes.

The more recipes you try, the more confidence you will have to attempt difficult or "fancy" cookies and desserts. Soon your loved ones will call you "the master of baking." After all, if you were able to learn how to read or write, baking will be a piece of cake!

I hope my book will erase the mysteries of baking and encourage you to replicate the recipes for yourself. And more importantly, I hope that you will soon develop your own little edible masterpieces. The only things you need are your will, determination, and time!

I wish you all the delights and happiness I have found in baking!

Baking Tools

You don't need many baking tools to make these cookies, but with the right ones, achieving the best results will be much easier. However, if you don't have all the tools, don't worry; you can always look for substitutes in your kitchen. Improvisation in cooking is everything.

1. **MIXING BOWLS** (plastic, ceramic, or glass) in a variety of sizes.

2. **SPOONS AND FORKS** to stir, fill, or decorate.

3. **PASTRY SPATULAS** to remove cookies from the pan without breaking them. If you don't have one, a flat-bladed flexible knife or a cheese cutter is a good substitute.

4. **FLOUR SIFTER** to decorate the finished cookies evenly with confectioners' sugar.

5. **COOLING RACK** to allow air to circulate around the cookies so they will cool quickly and evenly.

6. **ELECTRIC MIXER** with two types of beaters: regular beaters to mix, beat, and whip, and dough hooks to knead dough.

7. **PARCHMENT PAPER** to prevent cookies from sticking to the pan.

8. **CUTTING BOARDS** (wooden or plastic) to roll out dough and cutting dough.

9. **TOOTHPICKS** to use for decorating

10. **ROLLING PIN** (wooden or stone) to roll out cookie dough.

11. **ELECTRIC SCALE** to measure ingredients. These recipes will be more successful if you use a scale instead of measuring cups.

12. **BAKING SHEETS** or cookie pans to bake the cookies.

13. **COOKIE CUTTERS** to cut out different shapes. The basic cutters you will need are round, star, and heart shaped. But the more shapes you have, the more distinctive your cookies will be.

14. **PASTRY BRUSHES** to brush glazes and egg washes on cookies. Brushes with silicone bristles are good for large surfaces, and natural bristle brushes are the best for fragile dough and more precise work.

15. **VARIOUS PLASTIC SPATULAS** to remove cookies, sticky dough from bowls, etc.

Dark Chocolate

ONCE WHEN I WAS IN VENICE, ITALY, I DISCOVERED A HIDDEN CAFE WHERE I was served an amazing espresso. The waiter gave me the house specialty along with my coffee. It was a small square of very dark (or bittersweet) chocolate, and I was confused, because I expected a little cookie or biscuit. He explained to me that espresso and bittersweet chocolate harmonize extremely well. I took a bite of the dark chocolate. I let it melt a bit in my mouth, and then I took a sip of the coffee. I was not sure if I was doing it the right way, but after a few seconds, it felt like a small explosion of flavors in my mouth.

I bought a few of the chocolate squares and ate them while strolling through Venice's lovely alleys. They were delicious. The texture of the chocolate was surprisingly creamy after it started to melt, and the tiny touch of sweetness was a perfect balance to the bitterness. I actually felt for the very first time in my life, that I could appreciate real chocolate. From that point on, I have used only semisweet or bittersweet chocolate for all of my cookies, cakes, and desserts.

Bittersweet chocolate generally contains more chocolate liquor and less sugar than semisweet chocolate does. However, the percentage of cocoa in bittersweet chocolate may vary depending on the brand, so always read the ingredients. High quality chocolate should have at least 35 percent cacao solids or butter from cocoa beans. Some semisweet chocolate can contain up to 35 percent cocoa and can be used interchangeably with bittersweet. The higher the percentage of cocoa, the less sweet the chocolate will be, which is relevant in baking and decorating. Even a 65 percent chocolate tastes delicious to me. But once, I tasted a chocolate bar that was 99 percent cocoa, and it was so bitter that I was not able to eat it—not even a tiny sliver. Experiment with different percentages of cocoa to learn your cocoa limit.

Milk chocolate contains less cocoa solids and much more sugar than both semisweet and bittersweet chocolate. The sweet taste of this type of chocolate tends to suppress other flavors and can make cookies taste plain and overly sweet.

Dark chocolate, which includes both semisweet and bittersweet chocolates, harmonizes well with all kinds of ingredients and allows other flavors to develop. If you heat and prepare dark chocolate correctly, you can add a shiny, smooth topping on all your cakes and cookies.

White chocolate is made from sugar, milk, and cocoa butter or vegetable oil and has no cocoa solids. In my opinion, it is not a real chocolate. It is very sweet, which is why I rarely use it in doughs or fillings, but it is great for decoration. The white color makes a lovely contrast against dark chocolate.

How to Melt Chocolate

THERE ARE MANY FANCY WAYS TO MELT CHOCOLATE, BUT HERE ARE THE simplest and most effective methods that I use when I bake.

MICROWAVE

Microwaving is the quickest way to melt semisweet chocolate, but many people have difficulty doing it. Here are some simple tricks:

- Chop the chocolate into small bits (or use chocolate chips) and put them into a small microwave-safe dish.

- Choose a mid-level heat and put the chocolate in for about 10 seconds. The trick is to not let the chocolate get too hot. The temperature of the chocolate shouldn't get over 122°F (50°C). If the temperature gets too hot, the chocolate will burn and it will be unusable. Milk chocolate can burn at 113°F (45°C) and dark chocolate can be heated to 140°F (60°C) before it burns.

- Take the chocolate out of the microwave and stir it with a spoon. If it is not completely melted after stirring, it will need more time in the microwave.

- Put it in for another 10 seconds. Take the chocolate out and check by stirring again with a spoon. You want the consistency to be slightly creamy, but not totally melted.

- If there are little chunks in the chocolate, stir until they are all melted. At this point don't put the chocolate back in the microwave as it could burn.

HOT WATER (BAIN MARIE)

I RARELY USE THIS TECHNIQUE BECAUSE YOU RISK GETTING STEAM OR humidity into the chocolate, which makes it unusable for decorating. If you choose to use this method and steam gets in your chocolate, don't throw it away. It may be used for cookie fillings, dough, or sauces.

- Put a pot on the stovetop and fill it ¾ full with water. Using a candy thermometer, check to make sure that the water does not boil, but reaches a temperature of 98°F (37°C).

- Chop the chocolate into small bits (or use chocolate chips) and put them in a smaller pot. Then carefully set the smaller pot in the larger pot filled with the hot water. Alternatively, you may use a double boiler if you have one. The water temperature will melt the chocolate very gently, which lowers the risk of it burning.

- Stir the chocolate slowly, until it is almost melted. Then cool the chocolate as mentioned below.

How to Temper Chocolate

DARK CHOCOLATE HAS TO REACH A TEMPERATURE OF 90°F (32°C) BEFORE it can be used to decorate the cookies. By using either one of these methods mentioned above, you will get the perfect result. If the chocolate is not properly cooled, it will be too fluid and will not shine. The best way to cool or temper your chocolate is by stirring it continuously while adding a few chocolate chips or grated chocolate to the melted chocolate. Keep stirring until the chips are melted into the chocolate and it reaches the correct temperature, about 15 minutes. An alternate method is to leave the chocolate at room temperature and stir it from time to time until it is cool. However, the results are not as consistent with this method.

Paper Cones

PAPER CONES OR PIPING BAGS ARE SIMPLE BUT USEFUL TOOLS FOR SMALL cookie decorations. The cones may be used for tiny decorations that need to be very precise and accurate, and they are also great for larger jobs like filling cookies or cakes.

One of my favorite things about paper cones is that you can control the size of their tips by snipping more or less off of the ends. They are easy to make, but it might take you a few tries to make the perfect cone.

HOW TO MAKE A PAPER CONE:

1. Cut an 8-inch triangle out of parchment paper (or buy the pre-cut triangles).

2. Use your right hand to roll one of the points of the triangle to the center of the triangle, and with your left hand roll the bottom point up to complete the cone. The three points should overlap each other.

3. Adjust the cone, so that the point is completely closed and sharp.

4. Fold down the loose edges of the open end so it will not unroll.

5. Fill the cone with filling or icing. Fold the open ends several times, so that they are tightly closed.

6. Cut a small piece off of the tip of the cone. Hold the cone between your thumb and your other fingers. If the hole does not let the filling ease out, you can cut the tip again about $\frac{1}{4}$ inch or until it allows the filling to be piped onto the cookies.

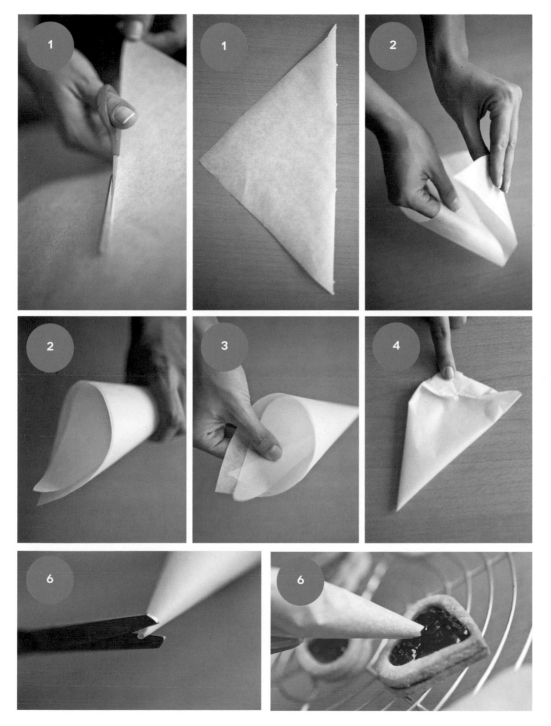

Vanilla Sugar

Vanilla sugar is a common ingredient of pastry recipes in European countries such as Germany, Finland, Austria, France, Hungary, Romania, and Slovenia. It can be difficult to obtain this specific sugar outside of Europe, but in America it can be found in import shops and grocery stores that cater to European populations. If you cannot find it locally, a replacement for vanilla sugar is pure vanilla extract. One teaspoon of vanilla extract equals two teaspoons of vanilla sugar, but I prefer to use vanilla sugar in my cooking for a more natural flavor.

Vanilla sugar is easy to make, and has no added artificial coloring or flavor. Vanilla beans might not be cheap, but they will pay off in flavor. This recipe yields a vanilla sugar that will keep for a long time and impart the scent and intense flavor of real vanilla in your cookies, cakes, coffee, or other foods or drinks. To intensify the flavor of this vanilla sugar, add a second vanilla bean.

MAKES 2 CUPS

1 WHOLE VANILLA BEAN
2 CUPS (400 GRAMS) GRANULATED SUGAR

1. Put the sugar in a one-quart glass storage container with a tight lid. Using a sharp knife, slice the vanilla bean lengthwise. With the side of the knife, scrape the insides of the bean into the container with the sugar. Cut the bean into two or three pieces and push them deep into the sugar with your fingers.

2. Seal the lid tightly and shake the jar until the vanilla flakes are visible and spread evenly through the sugar. Put the container on a dark shelf, and shake the jar vigorously every three days for two weeks. After two weeks the vanilla sugar is ready to be used.

> **BAKING TIP:** Do not remove the beans, as they will continue to flavor the sugar. Vanilla sugar is an original gift idea for the baking enthusiasts in your life.

Gingerbread Spice Mixture

Gingerbread—a confection made with honey or molasses and a specific mix of spices—is an especially popular snack in England, Scandinavia, Germany, Austria, Hungary, Poland, Croatia, and other European countries. It occurs in many different shapes and textures depending on the country in which it is made. The English version of gingerbread is denser, moister, and more like a sponge cake with raisins, nuts, apples, and other ingredients. The Middle and Eastern European gingerbread is rather a flat, semisoft biscuit cut into different shapes and served as a specialty at Christmas. Gingerbread houses are also very popular all over Europe. The dough and spices are similar to traditional gingerbread, but the density of the dough for the houses is much harder in order to make the construction more stable. The houses are decorated with brightly colored candies and nuts and are generally used only for decoration, though they are edible.

This recipe for Gingerbread Spice is not only good for gingerbread or ginger biscuits, but also for adding to waffle batter, muffins, cookies, or even ice cream. For a Christmassy morning brew, add one teaspoon of the mixture to ground coffee before brewing. The combination of the coffee and spice creates an amazingly rich flavor. If you can't find one of the spices, feel free to leave it out. As long as you have cinnamon, cloves, and anise the mixture will be close enough in flavor to the original recipe.

MAKES ABOUT ¾ CUP

½ CUP GROUND CINNAMON
1 TABLESPOON GROUND GINGER
1 TABLESPOON GROUND ALLSPICE
1 TEASPOON GROUND NUTMEG
1 TEASPOON GROUND CLOVES
1 TEASPOON GROUND ANISE SEED

1. Combine all of the above ingredients in a bowl and stir carefully with a long-handled spoon.

2. Scoop the mixture into a glass or ceramic jar with a tight-fitting lid. Store the mixture in the jar on a dark shelf for six months or more.

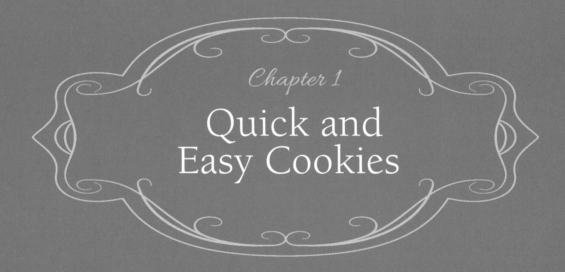

Chapter 1

Quick and Easy Cookies

Blueberry Surprise

Blueberries are one of my favorite berries, and that is the reason I created this recipe. I encourage cooks to use organic blueberries not only because they taste great, but also because they contain dietary fibers, vitamin C, vitamin A, calcium, magnesium, and resveratrol. Resveratrol is a natural compound found in many foods such as grapes and peanuts, and it is thought to protect against cancer and cardiovascular disease by acting as an antioxidant, anti-mutagen, and anti-inflammatory. Some studies have revealed that a blueberry-enriched diet can help people to lose weight and decrease belly fat, but I don't think these cookies have weight-reducing attributes.

MAKES ABOUT 3 DOZEN COOKIES

COOKIE DOUGH
2 CUPS (250 GRAMS) ALL-PURPOSE FLOUR
$2/3$ CUP (150 GRAMS) UNSALTED BUTTER, AT ROOM TEMPERATURE
$2/3$ CUP (70 GRAMS) CONFECTIONERS' SUGAR
2 MEDIUM EGG YOLKS
GRATED ZEST OF 1 LEMON

FILLING
$1/2$ CUP (70 GRAMS) FROZEN BLUEBERRIES

DECORATION
$1/3$ CUP (60 GRAMS) SEMISWEET CHOCOLATE CHIPS

1. **FOR THE COOKIE DOUGH:** Combine the dough ingredients in a bowl and, using the dough hook attachment of an electric mixer, knead until the dough is smooth, 3 to 5 minutes. Form the dough into a small loaf. Wrap the loaf in plastic wrap and let it rest in the refrigerator for about 30 minutes.

2. Preheat the oven to 350°F (180 °C).

3. Lightly flour a working surface and form the cookie dough into a log with a diameter of about $1/2$ inch (1 cm). With a knife, cut the dough into $1/2$-inch (1 cm) pieces and then form little balls out of each piece.

4. **FOR THE FILLING:** Flatten each of the balls and place one frozen blueberry in the middle. Then fold the dough over the fruit and form it again into a ball. Line a baking sheet with parchment paper, place the cookies on the sheet about 1 inch (2.5 cm) apart, and bake them for 15 minutes or until lightly golden. Carefully transfer the cookies to a cooling rack using a pastry spatula and allow them to cool completely.

5. **FOR THE DECORATION:** Melt the chocolate (see page 10), and use a teaspoon to pour a small drop on each cookie. These cookies are good for about two weeks stored in an airtight container at room temperature.

Chocolate Crescents

This is a variation of the Vanillekipferl *(Vanilla Crescent), which is well known in Germany, Austria, and Hungary. The origin of the vanilla crescent cookie dates back to the pagan times, but it became popular more recently due to a nineteenth-century German researcher. He discovered the synthetic substitution for the vanilla bean, which is the main ingredient for this biscuit, and he called it vanillin. Today it has become an integral part of a traditional Christian's Christmas baking. In my variation, the chocolate is dominant, which makes the taste totally different and surprisingly less sweet. It is a beloved tea or coffee biscuit that can be served all year long.*

MAKES ABOUT 6 DOZEN COOKIES

COOKIE DOUGH
1 CUP (170 GRAMS) SEMISWEET CHOCOLATE CHIPS
2$^{1}/_{2}$ CUPS (300 GRAMS) ALL-PURPOSE FLOUR
$^{1}/_{2}$ CUP (100 GRAMS) GRANULATED SUGAR
4 TABLESPOONS VANILLA SUGAR (SEE PAGE 14)
$^{3}/_{4}$ CUP (150 GRAMS) GROUND ALMONDS
2 STICKS (200 GRAMS) UNSALTED BUTTER, AT ROOM TEMPERATURE
1 MEDIUM EGG

DECORATION
1 CUP (100 GRAMS) SEMISWEET CHOCOLATE CHIPS

1. **FOR THE COOKIE DOUGH:** Melt the chocolate (see page 10). Combine the flour, granulated sugar, vanilla sugar, and ground almonds in the bowl of an electric mixer. Stir to mix and then add the butter and egg. Beat the dough with the dough hook attachment until it is smooth. Add the melted chocolate to the dough and beat it with the electric mixer until it is smooth, 3 to 5 minutes. Form the dough into a small loaf. Wrap the loaf in plastic wrap and let it rest in the refrigerator for about 1 hour.

2. Preheat the oven to 400°F (200°C).

3. Divide the dough into four equal portions and shape each portion into a roll that is about 9$^{3}/_{4}$ inches (25 cm) long. Using a sharp knife, cut the rolls into slices about $^{1}/_{2}$ inch (1 cm) thick and form the slices into balls. Roll the balls in your palm and form them into crescent or half-moon shapes.

4. Line a baking sheet with parchment paper and then place the crescents carefully on the pan about 1 inch (2.5 cm) apart. Bake the cookies for 8 to 10 minutes. Carefully transfer the cookies to a cooling rack using a pastry spatula and allow them to cool completely.

5. **FOR THE DECORATION:** Melt the chocolate (see page 10) and dip both ends of the crescents into the melted chocolate. Place the cookies back on the cooling rack and allow them to dry at room temperature. These cookies are good for about three weeks stored in an airtight container at room temperature.

Faux Pralines

Faux is a French word meaning "false" or "copied." I wanted to create a little treat that resembles the size and appearance of pralines without using chocolate. This light, lemony confectionery is a refreshing alternative to chocolate and candies that will not melt in the heat of summer. And because the pralines are wrapped in praline papers, they can be put into decorative boxes to be given away as unique gifts.

MAKES ABOUT 2 DOZEN COOKIES

COOKIE DOUGH
1$\frac{1}{2}$ STICKS (170 GRAMS) UNSALTED BUTTER, AT ROOM TEMPERATURE

$\frac{2}{3}$ CUP (75 GRAMS) CONFECTIONERS' SUGAR

1 MEDIUM EGG

$\frac{1}{2}$ TEASPOON LEMON JUICE

GRATED ZEST OF 1 LEMON

2 CUPS (250 GRAMS) ALL-PURPOSE FLOUR

2 TABLESPOONS HEAVY CREAM

FILLING
1 MEDIUM EGG WHITE

2 CUPS (200 GRAMS) CONFECTIONERS' SUGAR

3 TABLESPOONS LEMON MARMALADE OR LEMON JUICE

1. **FOR THE COOKIE DOUGH:** Beat the butter and sugar with an electric mixer until the dough is a smooth consistency, 3 to 5 minutes. Add the egg, lemon juice, and lemon zest and then add the flour one spoonful at a time. Beat until combined after adding each spoonful of flour. Add the heavy cream and mix the dough until it is a smooth consistency, 3 to 5 minutes.

2. Line a baking sheet with parchment paper. Fill a pastry bag with the cookie dough. Use a star-shaped tip and form about 60 small rosettes on the baking sheet about 1 inch (2.5 cm) apart. Put the filled sheet in the refrigerator for about 60 minutes.

3. Preheat the oven to 350°F (180°C).

4. Remove the rosettes from the refrigerator. Bake them in the oven for 12 to 15 minutes until they are lightly golden. Carefully transfer the cookies to a cooling rack using a pastry spatula and allow them to cool completely.

5. **FOR THE FILLING:** Beat the egg white with an electric mixer until it is semi-hard. Add the confectioners' sugar and whisk it until it becomes stiff and shiny, 3 to 5 minutes. Add the marmalade or lemon juice and stir it carefully into the egg white mixture with a wooden or plastic spoon.

6. Scoop the filling into a paper cone (see page 12), or use a teaspoon to fill the cookies.

7. Scoop a dab of filling onto a cooled-off cookie and cover it with a second cookie. You don't need to transfer them on a cooling rack, just simply put them on a plate or anything available in the kitchen.

8. Let the cookies dry for about 2 hours and then put them into small praline papers. Store them in an airtight container at room temperature. These cookies are good for about two weeks.

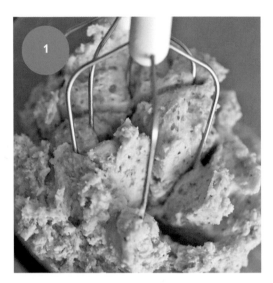

Jammed Cushions

This pastry is an adaptation of Hungarian Barátfüle, originally created by a German chef named Freund, who called his creation "Freund's filled pockets." Hungarians translated this into Barátfüle, which now literally means "friends' ear." The original pastry is a sweet dumpling filled with jam, cut into small triangles, and boiled. After cooking, the triangles are coated with fried breadcrumbs. This is the cookie version with the same pocket concept, but with a crunchy crust sprinkled with confectioners' sugar instead of breadcrumbs.

MAKES ABOUT 3 DOZEN COOKIES

COOKIE DOUGH

$2^1/_2$ CUPS (300 GRAMS) ALL-PURPOSE FLOUR

$2^1/_4$ STICKS (250 GRAMS) UNSALTED BUTTER, AT ROOM TEMPERATURE

$^1/_2$ CUP (125 GRAMS) SOUR CREAM OR HEAVY CREAM

FILLING

1 CUP (250 GRAMS) STRAWBERRY OR RASPBERRY JAM

DECORATION

$^1/_4$ CUP (28 GRAMS) CONFECTIONERS' SUGAR

1. **FOR THE COOKIE DOUGH:** Combine the dough ingredients in a bowl and, using the dough hook attachment of an electric mixer, knead until the dough is smooth, 3 to 5 minutes. Form the dough into a small loaf. Wrap the loaf in plastic wrap and let it rest in the refrigerator for about 3 hours.

2. Preheat the oven to 350°F (180°C).

3. Lightly flour a working surface and roll the dough out thinly, about $^1/_8$ inch (3 mm) thick. Using a sharp knife, cut the dough into $2^3/_4$ x $2^3/_4$-inch (7 x 7-cm) squares.

4. **FOR THE FILLING:** Fill each square with 1 teaspoon of the jam, brush the edges with water, and fold them into triangles. Using a fork, seal the edges of each square to make sure the jam will not leak.

5. Line a baking sheet with parchment paper and then use a pastry spatula to transfer the cookies carefully to the sheet about 1 inch (2.5 cm) apart. Bake the cookies for 15 minutes or until golden brown. Carefully remove them from the baking sheet with the pastry spatula and place them on a cooling rack.

6. **FOR THE DECORATION**: Sprinkle the warm cookies with confectioners' sugar. These cookies are good for about three weeks stored in an airtight container at room temperature.

BAKING TIP: The sour cream makes this dough more elastic, so it can be rolled thinner than other doughs.

Lemon Bars

This is the cookie version of a lemon cake. This simple, elegant dessert is a great recipe for home cooks who have little time for preparation, but a craving for sour lemony sweets. It is important that the lemon zest for the decoration is untreated and free of pesticides and wax. Look for organic lemons and wash the fruit carefully with hot water and then dry it with a towel. Use a zester or grater and make sure you do not grate so deep that you get the white portion under the zest. It is unpleasantly bitter in taste and will ruin the bars.

MAKES ABOUT 4 DOZEN COOKIES

COOKIE DOUGH
$3/4$ STICK (85 GRAMS) UNSALTED BUTTER, AT ROOM TEMPERATURE
$3/4$ CUP (80 GRAMS) CONFECTIONERS' SUGAR
1 MEDIUM EGG
$1/2$ TEASPOON GRATED LEMON ZEST
1 TABLESPOON LEMON JUICE
$1^{1}/4$ CUPS (150 GRAMS) ALL-PURPOSE FLOUR

DECORATION
$1^{1}/3$ CUPS (150 GRAMS) CONFECTIONERS' SUGAR
2 TO 3 TEASPOONS LEMON JUICE
GRATED ZEST OF 1 LEMON

1. **FOR THE COOKIE DOUGH:** Combine the dough ingredients in a bowl and, using the dough hook attachment of an electric mixer, knead until the dough is smooth, 3 to 5 minutes. Form the dough into a small loaf. Wrap the loaf in plastic wrap and let it rest in the refrigerator for about 30 minutes.

2. Preheat the oven to 350°F (170°C).

3. Lightly flour a working surface and roll the dough out thinly, about $1/8$ inch (3 mm) thick. Using a sharp knife, cut the dough into 2 x $3/4$-inch (5 x 2-cm) bars.

4. Line a baking sheet with parchment paper and then with a pastry spatula place the cookies carefully on the sheet about 1 inch (2.5 cm) apart. Bake the cookies for 10 to 13 minutes or until lightly golden. Carefully remove them from the baking sheet with the pastry spatula and place them on a cooling rack to cool completely.

5. **FOR THE DECORATION**: Mix the confectioners' sugar with the lemon juice until the mixture is creamy and thick. If it is stiff, simply add a few additional drops of lemon juice.

6. Using a teaspoon spread the sugar glaze onto the bars and sprinkle them with the grated lemon zest. These cookies are good for about three weeks stored in an airtight container at room temperature.

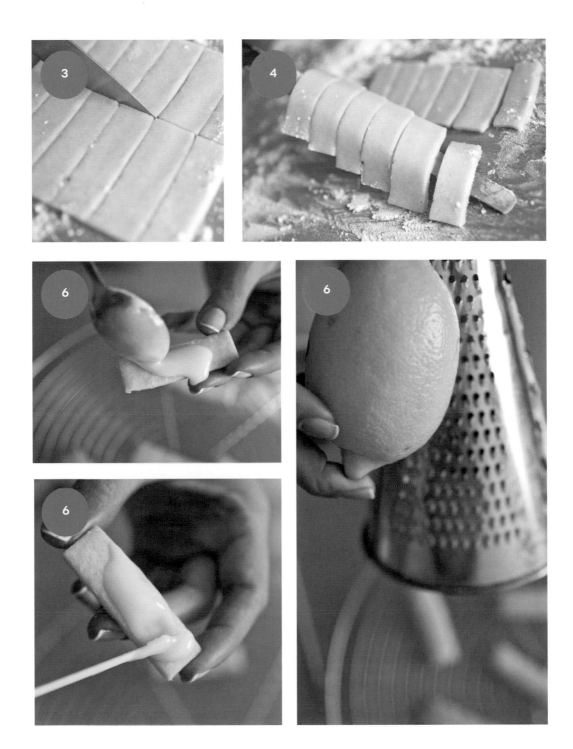

Orange Medallions

Oranges probably originated in Southeast Asia and were cultivated in China by 2500 BC. This delicious fruit contains many vitamins, such as vitamin C, calcium, and magnesium. The white part of the orange rind is very bitter and should not be used in cooking. For this recipe it is important that the orange is organic, untreated, and free of any pesticides and wax. Before the preparation, wash the fruit carefully with hot water and dry it with a towel.

MAKES ABOUT 6 DOZEN COOKIES

COOKIE DOUGH

$2^1\!/_2$ CUPS (300 GRAMS) ALL-PURPOSE FLOUR

$1^1\!/_2$ STICKS (170 GRAMS) UNSALTED BUTTER, AT ROOM TEMPERATURE

$^1\!/_2$ CUP (100 GRAMS) GRANULATED SUGAR

1 TABLESPOON VANILLA SUGAR (SEE PAGE 14)

1 MEDIUM EGG

2 TABLESPOONS ORANGE JUICE

DECORATION

$1^1\!/_2$ CUPS (175 GRAMS) CONFECTIONERS' SUGAR

4 TO 5 TABLESPOONS LEMON JUICE

$^1\!/_3$ CUP (60 GRAMS) SEMISWEET CHOCOLATE CHIPS

GRATED ZEST OF 1 ORANGE

1. **FOR THE COOKIE DOUGH:** Combine the dough ingredients in a bowl and, using the dough hook attachment of an electric mixer, knead until the dough is smooth, 3 to 5 minutes. Form the dough into a small loaf. Wrap the loaf in plastic wrap and let it rest in the refrigerator for about 30 minutes.

2. Preheat the oven to 350°F (175°C).

3. Lightly flour a working surface and roll the dough out thinly, about $^1\!/_8$ inch (3 mm) thick. Using a round cookie cutter about $1^1\!/_2$ inches (4 cm) in diameter, cut about 6 dozen cookies out of the dough, rerolling the scraps as necessary.

4. Line a baking sheet with parchment paper and then use a pastry spatula to place the cookies carefully on the sheet about 1 inch (2.5 cm) apart. Bake the cookies for 12 minutes or until lightly golden. Be sure to not let them turn brown. Carefully remove them from the baking sheet with the pastry spatula and place them on a cooling rack to cool completely.

5. **FOR THE DECORATION:** Mix the confectioners' sugar with the lemon juice. When the cookies are completely cooled, use a teaspoon to spread the sugar and lemon juice mixture on each cookie. Then place the glazed cookies back on the cooling rack.

6. Using the smallest holes in a grater on the skin of an orange, grate the orange zest directly onto the cookies.

These cookies are good for about three weeks stored in an airtight container at room temperature.

7. Melt the chocolate (see page 10). Dip a teaspoon into the melted chocolate and drizzle the chocolate over each cookie. The stripes do not have to be even, so be creative.

BAKING TIP: Longer and more uniform orange zests are possible if you grate in slower movements and if you rotate the orange while you grate it.

Poppy Seed Stars

Poppy seeds are not often used in American cuisine but are widely consumed in many parts of Central and Eastern Europe. There, sugared and ground poppy seeds are eaten with pasta, sprinkled on bread or pastries, or boiled with milk and used as a filling or topping for various kinds of pastries. Poppies have been grown as ornamental plants since 5000 BC. The flower's seeds—which are small and kidney-shaped, with a slate blue color and nutty flavor—have been used for centuries as a holistic remedy to aid sleep and to promote fertility and wealth. Here, they are mainly used for decoration, but you will definitely notice the pleasant aroma of this fascinating little seed. For this recipe you will need two cookie cutters: one star-shaped cutter about 2 inches (5 cm) in diameter, and one round cutter about ⅓ inch (8 mm) in diameter. (If you can't find a cookie cutter this small, you can use a drinking straw or clean pen cap.)

MAKES 18 COOKIES

COOKIE DOUGH
$1/2$ TEASPOON BAKING POWDER

2 TEASPOONS RUM OR ORANGE JUICE

$1^3/_4$ CUPS (220 GRAMS) ALL-PURPOSE FLOUR

5 TABLESPOONS (70 GRAMS) UNSALTED BUTTER, AT ROOM TEMPERATURE

1 MEDIUM EGG YOLK

$1/3$ CUP (70 GRAMS) VEGETABLE SHORTENING

1 TABLESPOON VANILLA SUGAR (SEE PAGE 14)

$1/2$ CUP (120 GRAMS) GRANULATED SUGAR

PINCH OF SALT

$1/4$ CUP (30 GRAMS) GROUND POPPY SEEDS

DECORATION
1 MEDIUM EGG WHITE

$1/3$ CUP (50 GRAMS) GOLD AND OFF-WHITE DECORATION SUGAR

FILLING
$1^1/_4$ CUPS (300 GRAMS) BLUEBERRY JAM

1. **FOR THE COOKIE DOUGH:** Dissolve the baking powder in the rum or orange juice in a bowl. Add the flour, butter, egg yolk, shortening, vanilla sugar, granulated sugar, and salt. Using the dough hook attachment of an electric mixer, knead until the dough is smooth, 3 to 5 minutes. Mix in the poppy seeds and form the dough into a small loaf. Wrap the loaf in plastic wrap and let it rest in the refrigerator for 30 to 60 minutes.

2. Lightly flour a working surface and roll the dough out thinly, 1/8 inch (3 mm) thick. Using the star-

shaped cookie cutter, cut the dough into approximately 36 stars. Using the small round cookie cutter or straw, punch a hole in the center of half of the stars. Keep the dough from the holes to make more cookies, or discard it.

3. Preheat the oven to about 350°F (180°C).

4. Line a baking sheet with parchment paper and then place the cookies carefully on the sheet with a pastry spatula.

5. **FOR THE DECORATION:** Whisk the egg white and with a brush spread it only on the cookies with a hole cut in the center. Sprinkle these cookies with the decoration sugar. Bake the cookies for 10 minutes, monitoring them closely, as the decoration sugar can burn easily. Carefully remove them from the baking sheet with the pastry spatula and place them on a cooling rack to cool completely.

6. **FOR THE FILLING:** Heat the jam in a microwave or in a pot on the stovetop until it becomes pourable. Spread one teaspoon of the jam on one side of each solid star cookie and then top each with a hole-centered cookie. If the holes are not completely filled with jam, scoop any remaining jam into a paper cone (see page 12) and pipe it in the gaps. These cookies are good for about three weeks stored in an airtight container at room temperature.

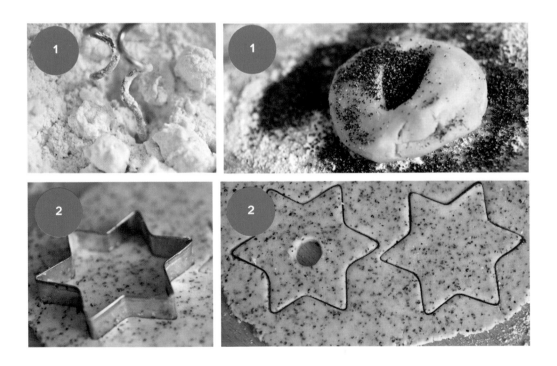

Red Dots

There are many names for this popular Christmas cookie—Hussarenkrapferl (Austrian), Kulleraugen (German), and Huszárcsók (Hungarian), for example—and just as many variations. This recipe is a combination of both Hungarian and German recipes. Hungarians usually don't use any decoration on the edges and Germans make them much bigger. The name "Hussar" refers to a type of light cavalry, which originated in Hungary in the fourteenth century. Their uniforms varied between territories and changed with time, but the dominant uniform color was red. Some say this cookie was named after them, and some say it has nothing to do with the Hussar. Regardless of what it is called, this cookie is a very delicious treat in many countries.

MAKES ABOUT 4 DOZEN COOKIES

COOKIE DOUGH
1½ STICKS (170 GRAMS) UNSALTED BUTTER, AT ROOM TEMPERATURE
⅓ CUP (114 GRAMS) HONEY
½ TEASPOON VANILLA SUGAR (SEE PAGE 14)
2 MEDIUM EGG YOLKS
2 CUPS (250 GRAMS) ALL-PURPOSE FLOUR

DECORATION
1 MEDIUM EGG WHITE
¼ CUP (50 GRAMS) DECORATION SUGAR

FILLING
3 TO 4 TABLESPOONS RED JAM

1. **FOR THE COOKIE DOUGH:** Whisk the butter, honey, vanilla sugar, and egg yolks in a medium-size bowl until the mixture is smooth, 3 to 5 minutes. Add the flour and, using the dough hook attachment of an electric mixer, knead until the dough is smooth, 3 to 5 minutes. Form the dough into a small loaf. Wrap the loaf in plastic wrap and put it in the refrigerator for about 30 minutes.

2. Lightly flour a working surface, form a log out of the dough about ³⁄4 inch (2-cm diameter), and wrap it in plastic wrap and put it in the refrigerator for another 30 minutes.

3. Remove the log from the refrigerator and place it on the working surface. Using a sharp knife, cut the log into approximately 48 ³⁄4-inch- (2-cm)-thick discs.

4. Line a baking sheet with parchment paper and then place the cookies carefully on the sheet with a pastry spatula, spacing them about 1 inch (2.5 cm) apart. Use the end of a wooden spoon to punch a hole in the center of each disc.

5. Preheat the oven to about 350°F (180°C).

6. **FOR THE DECORATION:** Whisk the egg white and use a pastry brush to spread it around the edge

of each cookie. Roll each of the cookies in the decoration sugar until all the edges of the discs are covered with the sugar.

7. Bake the cookies for 10 to 13 minutes or until lightly golden. Be sure to not let them turn brown. Carefully remove them from the baking sheet with the pastry spatula and place them on a cooling rack to cool completely.

8. **FOR THE FILLING:** When the cookies are cool, warm the jam in the microwave or in a small pot on the stovetop until it is pourable. Use a teaspoon measure or scoop some jam into a paper cone (see page 12) and fill the center of each cookie with jam. Let the cookies dry on a cooling rack. These cookies are good for about three weeks stored in an airtight container at room temperature.

Snow Squares

During one of my Christmas baking sessions, I created a quick and easy cookie that goes great with tea or coffee. Because of the baked egg white foam, this cookie is not only tasty but also fun to eat, as it is very crunchy. For a sweeter, fruity touch, use a dollop of jam to make crunchy sandwich cookies.

MAKES ABOUT 3 DOZEN COOKIES

COOKIE DOUGH
2 CUPS (250 GRAMS) ALL-PURPOSE FLOUR

$1^{1}/_{2}$ STICKS (150 GRAMS) UNSALTED BUTTER, AT ROOM TEMPERATURE

$^{3}/_{4}$ CUP (90 GRAMS) CONFECTIONERS' SUGAR

GRATED ZEST OF 1 LEMON

2 MEDIUM EGG YOLKS

TOPPING
2 MEDIUM EGG WHITES

$^{1}/_{3}$ CUP (70 GRAMS) GRANULATED SUGAR

JUICE OF $^{1}/_{2}$ LEMON

1 TABLESPOON VANILLA SUGAR (SEE PAGE 14)

$^{2}/_{3}$ CUP (80 GRAMS) CONFECTIONERS' SUGAR

1. **FOR THE COOKIE DOUGH.** Combine the dough ingredients in a bowl and, using the dough hook attachment of an electric mixer, knead until the dough is smooth, 3 to 5 minutes. Form the dough into a small loaf. Wrap the loaf in plastic wrap and let it rest in the refrigerator for about 30 minutes.

2. Preheat the oven to 320°F (160°C).

3. Place parchment paper on a working surface and sprinkle it lightly with flour. Roll the dough out to a $^{1}/_{8}$ inch (3 mm) thickness. Line a baking sheet with parchment paper and then transfer the uncut dough to the sheet and pre-bake it for 10 minutes. Remove the dough from the oven and let it cool on the baking sheet while preparing the topping.

4. **FOR THE TOPPING:** Beat the egg whites with an electric mixer until they are semi-firm. Gently pour the granulated sugar into the beaten egg whites and beat it together with a whisk. While continuously whisking, add the lemon juice, vanilla sugar, and confectioners' sugar. Keep whisking the mixture until it is shiny but firm.

5. Using a rubber spatula spread the egg white mixture about $^{1}/_{8}$ inch (3 mm) thick on the cooled pre-baked dough. Bake for 8 minutes. Carefully remove the baked dough from the baking sheet and place it on a cooling rack to cool completely.

6. Use a sharp knife to cut the baked dough into 1 x 1-inch (2.5 x 2.5-cm) squares. Since the topping is

semi-hard, the edges of the squares will be uneven and break while you cut them. This gives the cookies the "snow" effect. These cookies are good for about four weeks stored in an airtight container at room temperature.

BAKING TIP: Before serving, let the cookies sit for 24 hours so that the baked egg white topping will be crunchier.

BAKING TIP: Instead of cutting the dough into squares, you can use any shape (heart, bell, circle) cookie cutter you would like.

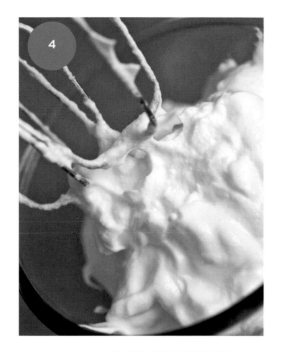

Sprinkled Flowers

This cookie contains sour cream, which is very typical for Middle and Eastern European recipes, but it apparently originated from Russia. The lightly sour flavor of the cream combined with sugar creates an exceptional flavor. Please don't use low-fat sour cream because the fat lipids in whole sour cream are an important flavor carrier that delivers taste and smell. According to Purdue University research, the human tongue seems to respond to the flavor of fats, not just sweet, salty, sour, bitter, and savory. This can explain why fat-free food is not usually satisfying. For this recipe you will need two round or flower-shaped cookie cutters: one that is about $1\frac{1}{2}$ inches (4 cm) in diameter and one that is about $\frac{1}{2}$ inch (1.25 cm) in diameter.

MAKES ABOUT 4 DOZEN COOKIES

COOKIE DOUGH

2 CUPS (250 GRAMS) ALL–PURPOSE FLOUR

$\frac{1}{4}$ CUP (60 GRAMS) SOUR CREAM

$1\frac{1}{2}$ STICKS (170 GRAMS) UNSALTED BUTTER, AT ROOM TEMPERATURE

DECORATION

1 MEDIUM EGG YOLK

1 TABLESPOON HEAVY CREAM

$\frac{1}{3}$ CUP (50 GRAMS) MULTICOLORED DECORATION SUGAR

1. **FOR THE COOKIE DOUGH:** Combine the dough ingredients in a bowl and, using the dough hook attachment of an electric mixer, knead until the dough is smooth, 3 to 5 minutes. Form the dough into a small loaf. Wrap the loaf in plastic wrap and let it rest in the refrigerator for about 60 minutes.

2. Lightly flour a working surface and roll the dough out thinly, about $\frac{1}{4}$ inch (6 mm) thick. Using the larger cookie cutter cut about 48 cookies out of the dough. Using the smaller cookie cutter cut out the center of each cookie. The dough may be re-rolled to form more cookies or discarded.

3. Preheat the oven to 350°F (175°C).

4. Line a baking sheet with parchment paper and then place the cookies carefully on the sheet with a pastry spatula, spacing them about 1 inch (2.5 cm) apart.

5. **FOR THE DECORATION:** Whisk together the egg yolk and heavy cream. Using a pastry brush spread the mixture on the top of each cookie and then sprinkle with decoration sugar.

6. Bake the cookies for 12 to 15 minutes. Carefully remove them from the baking sheet with the pastry spatula and place them on a cooling rack to cool completely. These cookies are good for about four weeks stored in an airtight container at room temperature.

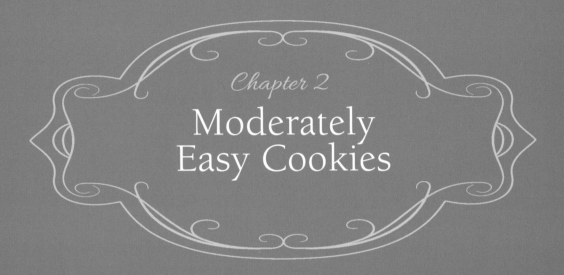

Chapter 2

Moderately
Easy Cookies

Apricot Rings

Easter customs vary among Christians all around the world, but decorating Easter eggs is a common tradition as is egg hunting and appearances by the Easter Bunny. Like many other Europeans, Hungarians celebrate this holiday by painting hard-boiled eggs and putting them into a basket filled with fake grass and flowers. Families tend to prepare too much food, so many of the colorful hard-boiled eggs remained uneaten. Frugal mothers devised new recipes to use the eggs, and this recipe is an example of their ingenuity. The boiled egg yolk in the rings gives the dough a silky texture without taking away its crunchiness. For this recipe you will need two round cookie cutters: one that is about $1\frac{1}{2}$ inches (4 cm) in diameter and one that is about $\frac{1}{2}$ inch (1.25 cm) in diameter.

MAKES ABOUT 4 DOZEN COOKIES

COOKIE DOUGH

3 HARD-BOILED EGG YOLKS

2 CUPS (250 GRAMS) ALL-PURPOSE FLOUR

$\frac{1}{4}$ CUP (60 GRAMS) GRANULATED SUGAR

GRATED ZEST OF 1 LEMON

1 TEASPOON LEMON JUICE

$2\frac{1}{2}$ STICKS (250 GRAMS) UNSALTED BUTTER, AT ROOM TEMPERATURE

DECORATION

1 EGG YOLK

1 TABLESPOON HEAVY CREAM

$\frac{1}{2}$ CUP (50 GRAMS) SLICED ALMONDS

FILLING

$\frac{1}{2}$ CUP (200 GRAMS) APRICOT MARMALADE

1. **FOR THE COOKIE DOUGH:** Grate the hard-boiled egg yolks into crumbles (or press them through a garlic press) and combine them with the flour in a medium-size bowl. Add the remaining dough ingredients and beat until the dough is smooth. Form the dough into a small disc, wrap it in plastic wrap, and let it rest in the refrigerator for about 30 minutes.

2. Lightly flour a work surface and roll the dough out thinly, about $\frac{1}{8}$ inch (3 mm) thick. Using the larger of the two cookie cutters cut 96 circles out of the dough. In the center of half of the circles, use the smaller cookie cutter to cut a smaller circle, making rings. You should have about 48 circles and 48 rings.

3. Preheat the oven to about 400°F (200°C).

4. Line a baking sheet with parchment paper and then transfer the rounds carefully to the pan with a pastry spatula. Bake the rounds for ten minutes, or until golden. Carefully remove them from the baking sheet with the pastry spatula and place them on a cooling rack to cool completely.

5. **FOR THE DECORATION:** Whisk together the egg yolk and heavy cream, brush the egg wash over the rings, and sprinkle them with the sliced almonds. Bake the rings for 10 minutes, or until lightly golden. Carefully remove them from the baking sheet with the pastry spatula and place them on a cooling rack to cool completely.

6. **FOR THE FILLING:** Spread about a teaspoon of marmalade on each cooled round. Gently press the rings over the rounds to make filled cookies. These cookies are good for about three weeks stored in an airtight container at room temperature.

Cat's Eyes

When I was a kid, I ate chocolate hazelnut spread with everything that I could find in the kitchen, including bananas, toast, crêpes, pasta, and hot milk. The first spread was called Supercrema. It was developed in 1951 and sold by an Italian confectionery. Later on, it became a huge success all over Europe, inspiring many cooks to create recipes for cakes and other desserts. Chocolate hazelnut spread can be rather sweet, but my addition of orange zest in this recipe brings a good balance. For this recipe you will need two cookie cutters: one circle cutter that is about $1\frac{1}{2}$ inches (4 cm) in diameter and one $\frac{1}{2}$ x $\frac{1}{2}$-inch square cutter.

MAKES ABOUT 3 DOZEN COOKIES

COOKIE DOUGH
2 CUPS (250 GRAMS) ALL-PURPOSE FLOUR

$1\frac{1}{2}$ STICKS (150 GRAMS) UNSALTED BUTTER, AT ROOM TEMPERATURE

$\frac{2}{3}$ CUP (70 GRAMS) CONFECTIONERS' SUGAR

2 MEDIUM EGG YOLKS

GRATED ZEST OF 1 ORANGE

FILLING
GRATED ZEST OF 1 ORANGE

$\frac{1}{2}$ CUP (150 GRAMS) HAZELNUT SPREAD

DECORATION
$\frac{1}{3}$ CUP (50 GRAMS) SEMISWEET CHOCOLATE

1. **FOR THE COOKIE DOUGH:** Combine the dough ingredients in a bowl and using the dough hook attachment of an electric mixer knead until the dough is smooth, 3 to 5 minutes. Form the dough into a small loaf. Wrap the loaf in plastic wrap and let it rest in the refrigerator for about 30 minutes.

2. Preheat the oven to 350°F (180°C).

3. Lightly flour a working surface and roll the dough out thinly, about $\frac{1}{8}$ inch (3mm) thick. Using the circular cookie cutter cut the dough into about 60 cookies. Then, using the $\frac{1}{2}$-inch square cutter, cut out a square from the middle of half the circles. Use a toothpick to remove the squares, which can be rolled for additional cookies or discarded.

4. Line a baking sheet with parchment paper and then transfer the rounds carefully to the sheet with a pastry spatula. Bake the cookies for 15 minutes or until lightly golden. Carefully remove them from the baking sheet with the pastry spatula and place them on a cooling rack to cool completely.

5. **FOR THE FILLING:** Stir together the orange zest and hazelnut spread. Spread a teaspoonful of the hazelnut mixture on the rounds and then top the cookies with the cutout center.

6. FOR THE DECORATION: Melt the chocolate (see page 10) and use a teaspoon to drizzle the melted chocolate in parallel lines on each cookie. The lines can be of varying widths, so be creative. These cookies are good for about three weeks stored in an airtight container at room temperature.

Chocolate Nougat Surprise

When people see this cookie with chocolate and hazelnuts on the top, they don't expect it to be filled with anything. But the surprise is the creamy and tasty chocolate nougat in the middle of the biscuit. This dough is also perfect for many kinds of fillings, like dried fruits, nuts, or your favorite chocolate, but it is also very tasty when eaten plain. This recipe is a great opportunity to experiment and create your very own custom made cookie.

MAKES ABOUT 4 DOZEN COOKIES

COOKIE DOUGH
$1^1/_8$ STICKS (130 GRAMS) UNSALTED BUTTER, AT ROOM TEMPERATURE

$^1/_2$ CUP (100 GRAMS) GRANULATED SUGAR

1 MEDIUM EGG

2 MEDIUM EGG YOLKS

2 CUPS (250 GRAMS) ALL-PURPOSE FLOUR

1 TEASPOON BAKING POWDER

FILLING
7 OUNCES (200 GRAMS) CHOCOLATE NOUGAT

$1^1/_2$ TEASPOONS GROUND CINNAMON

1 TEASPOON GRATED ORANGE ZEST

DECORATION
$^2/_3$ CUP (100 GRAMS) SEMISWEET CHOCOLATE CHIPS

2 TABLESPOONS CHOPPED HAZELNUTS

1. **FOR THE COOKIE DOUGH:** Beat the butter and sugar using the paddle attachment of an electric mixer until the mixture resembles a smooth paste, 3 to 5 minutes. Add the egg, egg yolks, flour, and baking powder and beat until the dough is smooth, 3 to 5 minutes. Form the dough into a small loaf. Wrap the loaf in plastic wrap and let it rest in the refrigerator for about 30 to 60 minutes.

2. **FOR THE FILLING:** Stir together the nougat, cinnamon, and orange zest. Form the filling with your fingers into 48 1-inch balls.

3. Preheat the oven to 350°F (180°C).

4. **TO ASSEMBLE THE COOKIES:** Put one teaspoon of the cookie dough in your palm and form it into a small ball. Flatten the ball with your fingers and place a nougat ball in the center. Wrap the dough around the ball in the shape of a football. Put the cookies in the refrigerator for 60 minutes so they will keep their shape during baking.

5. Remove the cookies from the refrigerator. Line a baking sheet with parchment paper and then place the cookies carefully on the sheet with a pastry spatula. Bake the cookies for 10 minutes or until lightly

golden. Be sure to not let them turn brown. Carefully remove them from the baking sheet with the pastry spatula and place them on a cooling rack to cool completely.

6. **FOR THE DECORATION:** Melt the chocolate (see page 10). Dip a teaspoon into the chocolate and drizzle it over the cookies. The stripes don't have to be even. Sprinkle the chopped nuts over the warm chocolate. These cookies are good for about four weeks stored in an airtight container at room temperature.

BAKING TIP: If you can't find chocolate nougat, you can use chocolate chips.

BAKING TIP: Another variation is to not decorate the cookies. Before serving them, put 5 or 6 cookies in the microwave for 5 to 10 seconds. Remove the cookies from the microwave and sprinkle them with confectioners' sugar. This will make the filling even more gooey and more of a surprise when someone bites into them.

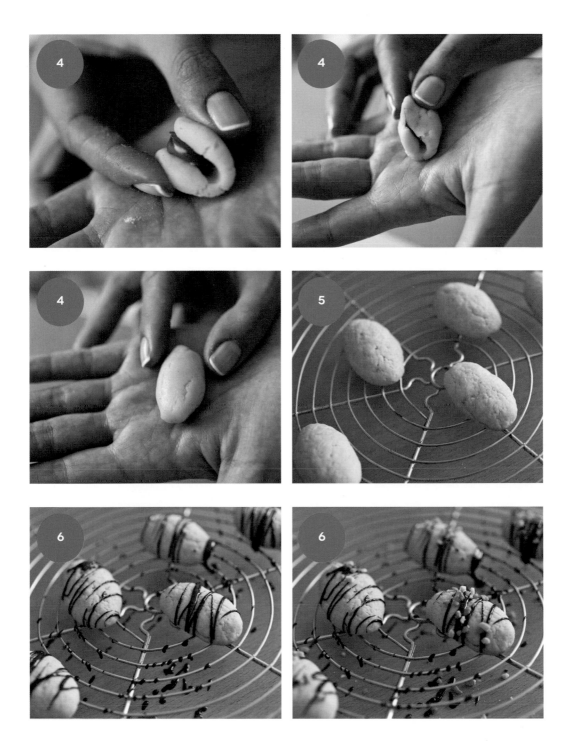

Coconut Clouds

The coconut is technically not a nut, but a drupe or stone fruit. A drupe is a fruit with an outer fleshy part that surrounds a shell with a seed inside it. Examples of drupes are mangos, olives, coffee seeds, pistachio nuts, peaches, plums, cherries, and many more. The origin of the plant is subject to debate, but the oldest fossils of the modern coconut—which were found in Australia and India—date from around 37 million years old. One of the earliest mentions of the coconut appeared in the 1280 journals of Marco Polo, in which he called the coconut, the "nux indica." For this recipe you will need two round cookie cutters: one that is 1½ inches (4 cm) in diameter and one that is ½ inch (1.3 cm) in diameter.

MAKES ABOUT 4 DOZEN COOKIES

COOKIE DOUGH
2 CUPS (250 GRAMS) ALL-PURPOSE FLOUR

½ TEASPOON BAKING POWDER

⅓ CUP (75 GRAMS) GRANULATED SUGAR

1 TABLESPOON VANILLA SUGAR (SEE PAGE 14)

2 MEDIUM EGG YOLKS

1 STICK (115 GRAMS) UNSALTED BUTTER, AT ROOM TEMPERATURE

FILLING
3 MEDIUM EGG WHITES

⅔ CUP (150 GRAMS) GRANULATED SUGAR

1½ CUPS (175 GRAMS) UNSWEETENED COCONUT FLAKES

ADDITIONAL INGREDIENTS
1 MEDIUM EGG YOLK

1 TABLESPOON MILK

1. **FOR THE COOKIE DOUGH:** Combine the dough ingredients in a bowl and, using the dough hook attachment of an electric mixer, knead until the dough is smooth, 3 to 5 minutes. Form the dough into a small loaf. Wrap the loaf in plastic wrap and let it rest in the refrigerator for about 30 minutes.

2. Lightly flour a working surface and roll the dough out thinly, about ⅛ inch (3 mm) thick. Using the two round cookie cutters, cut 1½-inch (4-cm) circles out of half of the dough and cut ½-inch (1.3-cm) circles out of the other half of the dough. You should have about 48 of each size cookie.

3. Preheat the oven to about 400°F (200°C).

4. Line a baking sheet with parchment paper and then transfer the larger circles carefully to the sheet with a pastry spatula.

5. FOR THE FILLING: Whip the egg whites with an electric mixer until firm and then slowly add the sugar. Mix the filling until it becomes shiny but stiff. Using a large wooden spoon, gently fold in the coconut flakes.

6. Place 2 teaspoons of filling (the "clouds") on the unbaked larger cookies and then place the smaller $\frac{1}{2}$-inch (1.3-cm) unbaked cookies on top of the filling.

7. Whisk together the egg yolk and the milk, and brush the egg wash over the smaller cookies. Bake the cookies for 10 to 15 minutes or until lightly golden. Be sure to not let them turn brown. Carefully remove them from the baking sheet with the pastry spatula and place them on a cooling rack to cool completely. These cookies are good for about three weeks stored in an airtight container at room temperature.

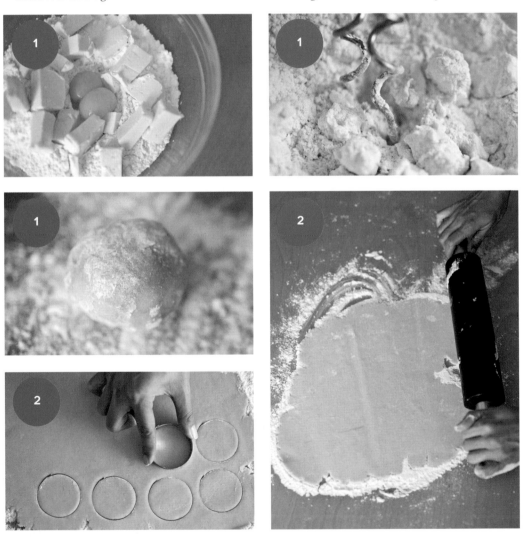

Gingerbread Bites

The term gingerbread originates from the Latin word zingiber, *which refers to preserved ginger added to a confection made with honey and spices. The first evidence of spiced honey cakes dates back to 350 BC, when they were buried with Egyptian royalty to be eaten in the afterlife. Gingerbread as we know it today was invented in Belgium in the tenth century and spread throughout European countries during the thirteenth century. It is a very popular snack today in England, Scandinavia, Germany, Austria, Hungary, Poland, and Croatia.*

MAKES ABOUT 1¹/₂ DOZEN COOKIES

COOKIE DOUGH

²/₃ CUP (225 GRAMS) HONEY

5 TABLESPOONS (70 GRAMS) UNSALTED BUTTER, AT ROOM TEMPERATURE

2 CUPS (250 GRAMS) ALL-PURPOSE FLOUR

1 TEASPOON BAKING POWDER

²/₃ CUP (100 GRAMS) CHOPPED ALMONDS

1 TABLESPOON GINGERBREAD SPICE MIXTURE (SEE PAGE 15)

FILLING

ABOUT 20 CANNED (UNSWEETENED) OR FRESH PITTED CHERRIES

DECORATION

¹/₄ CUP (50 GRAMS) APRICOT JAM

³/₄ CUP (100 GRAMS) GRATED CHOCOLATE OR CHOCOLATE SPRINKLES

1. **FOR THE COOKIE DOUGH:** Melt the honey and butter into a medium nonstick pan over medium heat. Add the flour, baking powder, almonds, and spice mixture; mix them together with a fork. Remove the pan from the heat.

2. Preheat the oven to 350°F (176°C).

3. While the dough is still warm, form small balls in your palm and then flatten them. If the mixture gets too sticky, sprinkle confectioners' sugar on your palms.

4. **FOR THE FILLING:** Put a cherry into each flattened cookie and wrap the dough around it. Continue until all the dough is used. You should have about 18 cookies.

5. Line a baking sheet with parchment paper and then place the cookies carefully on the pan with a pastry spatula, spacing them about 1 inch (2.5 cm) apart. Bake the cookies for 15 minutes or until lightly golden. Be sure to not let them turn brown. Carefully remove them from the baking sheet with the pastry spatula and place them on a cooling rack to cool completely.

6. **FOR THE DECORATION:** When the cookies are cool, warm the apricot jam in a saucepan on the stove. Brush a teaspoon of jam onto each cookie. Roll the cookies in the grated chocolate or the chips. These cookies are good for about two weeks stored in an airtight container at room temperature.

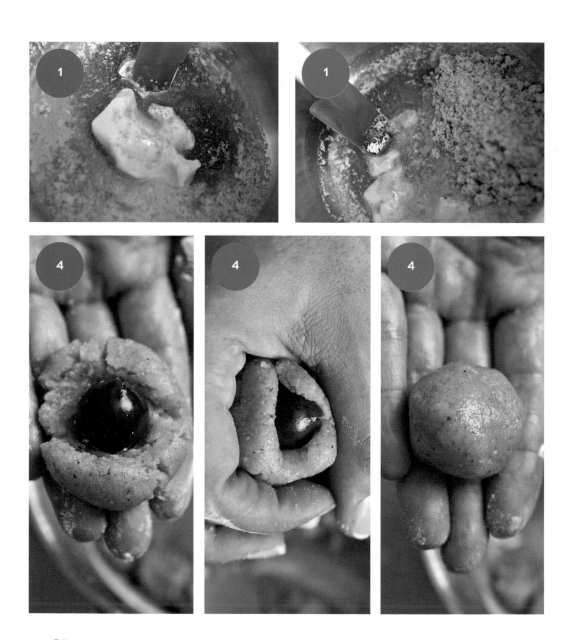

Hearts and Stars Linzer Cookies

The word Linzer refers to "Linzer Torte," one of the oldest tart recipes, which is named after Linz, the third largest city in Austria. The city of Linz is historically known for its vibrant music and arts scene and became the European capital of culture in 2009. The Linzer Torte is a crumbly pastry filled with thick plum or raspberry jam and covered with a dough lattice. This cookie employs a similar recipe as the tart, but the dough is cut into different shapes. The top cookies traditionally have small circles in the center, known as "Linzer Eyes." These cookies are also common in Germany and Hungary. For this recipe you will need sets of larger and smaller cookie cutters: one star-shaped and the second heart-shaped, each about $1\frac{1}{2}$ inches (4 cm) in diameter, and smaller star and heart cookie cutters, each about $\frac{1}{2}$ inch (1.5 cm) in diameter.

MAKES ABOUT 5 DOZEN COOKIES

COOKIE DOUGH
$4\frac{1}{8}$ CUPS (500 GRAMS) ALL-PURPOSE FLOUR

2 STICKS PLUS 5 TABLESPOONS (300 GRAMS) UNSALTED BUTTER, AT ROOM TEMPERATURE

$1\frac{1}{3}$ CUPS (150 GRAMS) CONFECTIONERS' SUGAR

3 MEDIUM EGG YOLKS

GRATED ZEST OF 1 LEMON

FILLING
$\frac{3}{4}$ CUP (200 GRAMS) APRICOT JAM

$\frac{3}{4}$ CUP (200 GRAMS) STRAWBERRY JAM

DECORATION
$1\frac{1}{3}$ CUPS (150 GRAMS) CONFECTIONERS' SUGAR

1. **FOR THE COOKIE DOUGH:** Combine the dough ingredients in a bowl and, using the dough hook attachment of an electric mixer, knead until the dough is smooth, 3 to 5 minutes. Form the dough into a small loaf. Wrap the loaf in plastic wrap and let it rest in the refrigerator for about 30 minutes.

2. Lightly flour a working surface and roll the dough out thinly, about $\frac{1}{8}$ inch (3 mm) thick. Using the larger star- and heart-shaped cookie cutters cut out 60 cookies of each shape. Using the smaller star- and heart-shaped cookie cutters, cut the centers out of half of the correspondingly shaped cookies. Remove the inside dough from the small heart- and star-shaped cookies with a toothpick. Use the inside dough to make additional cookies or discard it.

3. Preheat the oven to 350°F (175°C).

4. Line a baking sheet with parchment paper and then transfer the cookies carefully to the sheet with a

pastry spatula. Bake the cookies for 5 to 10 minutes or until lightly golden. Be sure to not let them turn brown, as the cut-out cookies will cook faster than the whole cookies. Carefully remove them from the baking sheet with the pastry spatula and place them on a cooling rack to cool completely.

5. **FOR THE FILLING:** Heat the two types of jam separately in the microwave or in pots on a stovetop until they are pourable. Spread the jam lightly with a pastry brush over each solid cookie (strawberry jam for the hearts and apricot jam for the stars) and cover each with a correspondingly shaped cut-out cookie top.

6. **FOR THE DECORATION:** Dust each assembled cookie with confectioners' sugar.

7. Fill the cookies centers full of the jam using a small spoon or a paper cone (see page 12). These cookies are good for about two weeks stored in an airtight container at room temperature.

BAKING TIP: You can use any type of jam you prefer.

Marzipan Kisses

This recipe is based on one of Spain's specialties, marzipan, an almond paste that was the most famous dessert in Toledo (South Spain, Andalusia) and also known as an aphrodisiac in early 850–900. This cookie is sweet because of all the marzipan, but it is a moist and flavorful treat. If you like marzipan, you will love this recipe! Today, there are many marzipan-based cakes and cookies all over Europe, which are all absolutely delicious. This one is also called "Bethmännchen" and is a specialty from Frankfurt, Germany. Yet, some people today claim that a Parisian confectioner invented this cookie in 1838.

MAKES ABOUT 3 DOZEN COOKIES

COOKIE DOUGH

$2/3$ CUP (70 GRAMS) CONFECTIONERS' SUGAR

7 OUNCES (200 GRAMS) MARZIPAN

1 MEDIUM EGG

3 TEASPOONS ALL–PURPOSE FLOUR

$1/2$ CUP (70 GRAMS) GROUND ALMONDS

DECORATION

1 MEDIUM EGG YOLK

1 TABLESPOON HEAVY CREAM

$2/3$ CUP (100 GRAMS) WHOLE SKINLESS ALMONDS

1. **FOR THE COOKIE DOUGH:** Combine the dough ingredients in a bowl and, using the dough hook attachment of an electric mixer, knead until the dough is smooth, 3 to 5 minutes.

2. Form the dough into 1-inch (2.5 cm) balls. Add confectioners' sugar as necessary to keep the balls from sticking to your hands.

3. Line a baking sheet with parchment paper and then transfer the cookies carefully to the sheet about 1 inch (2.5 cm) apart.

4. **FOR THE DECORATION:** In a small bowl, whisk the egg yolk with the heavy cream. Use a soft brush to spread the glaze on the balls.

5. Preheat the oven to 320°F (160°C).

6. Carefully cut the almonds in half with a knife. Press three of the almond halves into the top of each cookie. Bake the cookies for 15 minutes or until lightly golden. Carefully remove them from the baking sheet with the pastry spatula and place them on a cooling rack to cool completely. These cookies are good for about four weeks stored in an airtight container at room temperature.

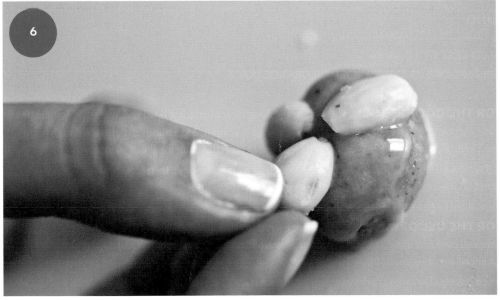

Princess Cookies

This cookie's flavor is dominated by two aromatic ingredients: marzipan and Grand Marnier, which was created in France in 1880 and is a blend of true cognacs and distilled essence of bitter orange. In addition to popular cocktails such as the B-52 and the Dirty Harry, this liqueur is used in several kinds of pastries, such as cream puffs, crêpes, and crème brûlée. For this recipe you will need one round cookie cutter that is about $1\frac{1}{4}$ inches (3 cm) in diameter.

MAKES ABOUT 1½ DOZEN COOKIES

COOKIE DOUGH

4 CUPS (500 GRAMS) ALL-PURPOSE FLOUR

$2\frac{1}{2}$ STICKS (300 GRAMS) UNSALTED BUTTER, AT ROOM TEMPERATURE

$1\frac{1}{3}$ CUPS (150 GRAMS) CONFECTIONERS' SUGAR

3 MEDIUM EGG YOLKS

GRATED ZEST OF 1 LEMON

DECORATION

1 MEDIUM EGG WHITE

3 TABLESPOONS GRANULATED SUGAR

3 TEASPOONS GROUND CINNAMON

$\frac{3}{4}$ CUP (100 GRAMS) SLICED ALMONDS

FILLING

$10\frac{1}{2}$ OUNCES (300 GRAMS) MARZIPAN

GRATED ZEST OF 1 ORANGE

3 TABLESPOONS GRAND MARNIER OR ORANGE JUICE

1. **FOR THE COOKIE DOUGH:** Combine the dough ingredients in a bowl and, using the dough hook attachment of an electric mixer, knead until the dough is smooth, 3 to 5 minutes. Form the dough into a small loaf. Wrap the loaf in plastic wrap and let it rest in the refrigerator for about 30 minutes.

2. Lightly flour a working surface and roll the dough out thinly, about $\frac{1}{8}$ inch (3 mm) thick. Using the round cookie cutter, cut the dough into approximately 36 cookies.

3. Preheat the oven to 350°F (175°C).

4. **FOR THE DECORATION:** Whisk the egg white and use a pastry brush to spread it on half of the unbaked cookies (about 18). Sprinkle the egg-washed cookies with the sugar and cinnamon, and place the sliced almonds on top of them.

5. Line a baking sheet with parchment paper and then transfer the cookies carefully to the pan with a pastry spatula. Bake the cookies for 10 to 15 minutes or until lightly golden. Be sure to not let them turn brown. Carefully remove them from the baking sheet with the pastry spatula and place them on a cooling rack to cool completely.

6. FOR THE FILLING: grate the marzipan into a bowl and add the orange zest and the liqueur or orange juice. Stir the filling with a fork until it is spreadable (it will still be very sticky).

7. Scoop the filling into a paper cone (see page 12) or simply use a teaspoon to spread it on the plain cookies; cover the filling with the decorated cookies. These cookies are good for about three weeks stored in an airtight container at room temperature.

Raisin Baskets

I love to snack on nuts and dried fruits when I get hungry in between meals. One day, while baking cookies, I had a craving for almonds. But the only ones I could find in the house were chopped. I had a small amount of leftover dough to give me inspiration, so I started looking for potential ingredients that would satisfy my craving. After several combinations, differing shapes, and some failed results, these cute little baskets were the end result. They have less sugar and more dietary fibers than most cookies due to the raisins and almonds, so you could even call them healthy! The almonds are a rich source of vitamin E and vitamin B, essential minerals, and monosaturated fats such as omega-6 and omega-9 fatty acids. The raisins have natural sugar and, like prunes and apricots, contain many antioxidants.

MAKES ABOUT 3 DOZEN COOKIES

COOKIE DOUGH
1 ⅔ CUPS (200 GRAMS) ALL-PURPOSE FLOUR

½ CUP (100 GRAMS) GRANULATED SUGAR

2 TABLESPOONS VANILLA SUGAR (SEE PAGE 14)

1 STICK (115 GRAMS) UNSALTED BUTTER, AT ROOM TEMPERATURE

2 MEDIUM EGG YOLKS

FILLING
⅔ CUP (100 GRAMS) RAISINS

1 TEASPOON RUM OR ORANGE JUICE

1 MEDIUM EGG YOLK

1 TEASPOON HEAVY CREAM

¼ CUP (30 GRAMS) CHOPPED ALMONDS

GRATED ZEST OF 1 ORANGE

ADDITIONAL INGREDIENTS
1 MEDIUM EGG WHITE

1. **FOR THE COOKIE DOUGH:** Combine the dough ingredients in a bowl and, using the dough hook attachment of an electric mixer, knead until the dough is smooth, 3 to 5 minutes. Form the dough into a small loaf. Wrap the loaf in plastic wrap and let it rest in the refrigerator for about 60 minutes.

2. **FOR THE FILLING:** Using a sharp knife dice the raisins and put them in a medium-size bowl. Add the rum or orange juice, egg yolk, heavy cream, almonds, and orange zest and then stir with a fork.

3. Preheat the oven to 350°F (175°C).

4. Lightly flour a working surface and roll the dough out thinly, about ⅛ inch (3 mm) thick. Using a round cookie cutter that is about 2 inches (5 cm) in diameter, cut the dough into about 36 cookies.

5. Line a baking sheet with parchment paper and then transfer the cookies carefully to the sheet with a pas-

try spatula, spacing them about 1 inch (2.5 cm) apart. Whisk the egg white and use a pastry brush to spread it around the edges of each cookie. Place $\frac{1}{2}$ teaspoon of the filling in the middle of each cookie. Use your fingers to form the cookie into the shape of a three cornered hat around the filling.

6. Bake the cookies for 15 minutes or until lightly golden. Be sure to not let them turn brown. Carefully remove them from the baking sheet with the pastry spatula and place them on a cooling rack to cool completely. These cookies are good for about three weeks stored in an airtight container at room temperature.

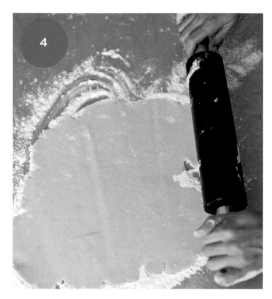

Sweet Bites

This cookie belongs to the pastry family Teegebäck, meaning "tea pastry," which originated in Germany. It is usually served with tea but is also tasty with milk or hot chocolate. Some people dip this cookie into their beverage before eating them so the crunchy biscuit becomes soft and the vanilla sugar melts into the cookie, enhancing its flavor.

MAKES ABOUT 7 DOZEN COOKIES

COOKIE DOUGH

$2^3/_4$ CUPS (330 GRAMS) ALL-PURPOSE FLOUR

2 STICKS (230 GRAMS) UNSALTED BUTTER, AT ROOM TEMPERATURE

1 CUP (100 GRAMS) CONFECTIONERS' SUGAR

$1/_3$ CUP (40 GRAMS) CORNSTARCH

4 MEDIUM EGG YOLKS

DECORATION

4 TABLESPOONS VANILLA SUGAR (SEE PAGE 14)

1 CUP (200 GRAMS) GRANULATED SUGAR

1. **FOR THE COOKIE DOUGH:** Combine the dough ingredients in a bowl and, using the dough hook attachment of an electric mixer, knead until the dough is smooth, 3 to 5 minutes. Form the dough into five or six rolls $1/_4$ inch (2.5 cm) in diameter. Wrap the rolls in plastic wrap and let them rest in the refrigerator for about 2 hours.

2. Preheat the oven to 350°F (175°C).

3. Remove the dough rolls from the refrigerator and cut them into $1/_2$-inch (1-cm) pieces. Form the pieces into 1-inch shapes, such as crescents, spirals, pretzels, or simple sticks out of the dough. Let your imagination go wild!

4. Line a baking sheet with parchment paper and then transfer the shapes carefully to the sheet with a pastry spatula, spacing them about 1 inch (2.5 cm) apart. Sprinkle 2 tablespoons of vanilla sugar on the cookies and bake for 13 minutes or until lightly golden. Be sure to not let them turn brown. Carefully remove them from the baking sheet with the pastry spatula and place them on a cooling rack.

5. **FOR THE DECORATION:** In a shallow bowl or on a plate mix the remaining vanilla sugar with the granulated sugar. Press the warm cookies into the sugar. These cookies are good for about five weeks stored in an airtight container at room temperature.

BAKING TIP: You can add cinnamon, ground hazelnuts, unsweetened coconut, or ground pistachio nuts to the sugar to create a variety of different flavors and designs.

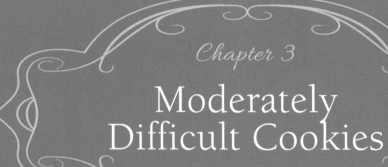

Chapter 3

Moderately
Difficult Cookies

Butter Rings

Like the French used to say, butter makes everything better. Nobody knows exactly where and when butter was first produced, but one of its oldest representations was found in a Greek mosaic dated 3000 BC. Butter became an essential ingredient for cooking, but its main use was in baking. Nothing tastes like it, and so it doesn't lend well to substitutions—not even margarine. This recipe was originally made with lard instead of butter, which was delicious. But in the last hundred years, as it was deemed unhealthy, lard fell out of fashion and many recipes in Europe were altered accordingly. For this recipe you will need two round cookie cutters: one that is about $1\frac{3}{4}$ inches (4.5 cm) in diameter and one that is about $\frac{1}{2}$ inch (1.5 cm) in diameter.

MAKES ABOUT 2 DOZEN COOKIES

COOKIE DOUGH
$1\frac{3}{4}$ CUPS (210 GRAMS) ALL-PURPOSE FLOUR
$\frac{1}{4}$ CUP (60 GRAMS) GRANULATED SUGAR
$1\frac{1}{4}$ STICKS (145 GRAMS) UNSALTED BUTTER, AT ROOM TEMPERATURE
2 MEDIUM EGG YOLKS

TOPPING
1 MEDIUM EGG WHITE
$\frac{3}{4}$ CUP (80 GRAMS) CONFECTIONERS' SUGAR

FILLING
$\frac{1}{2}$ CUP (140 GRAMS) STRAWBERRY JAM

1. **FOR THE COOKIE DOUGH:** Combine the dough ingredients in a bowl and, using the dough hook attachment of an electric mixer, knead until the dough is smooth, 3 to 5 minutes. Form the dough into a small loaf. Wrap the loaf in plastic wrap and let it rest in the refrigerator for about 30 minutes.

2. Lightly flour a work surface and roll the dough out thinly, about $\frac{1}{8}$ inch (3 mm) thick. Using the larger cookie cutter cut the dough into 48 circles. With half of the dough circles, use the smaller cookie cutter to punch out the centers and make rings. You should have about 24 each of circles and rings.

3. Preheat the oven to about 400°F (200°C).

4. Line two baking sheets with parchment paper and then transfer the circles carefully to one of the baking sheets with a pastry spatula. Transfer the rings to the second baking sheet; set aside. Bake the circles for about 8 minutes. Bake the rings in step 6.

5. **FOR THE TOPPING:** Whip the egg white with an electric mixer until it is almost thick, about 2 minutes on high speed. Add the confectioner's sugar and beat it until it makes a thick and shiny frosting, about 10 minutes on medium-high speed.

6. Scoop the frosting into a piping bag with a round piping tip, and decorate the unbaked rings. Bake the rings for 8 to 12 minutes, making sure that the frosting stays white and does not brown. Carefully remove them from the baking sheet with the pastry spatula and place them on a cooling rack to cool completely.

7. **FOR THE FILLING:** Brush the circles with jam and cover with the egg white–covered rings. Fill the center of the cookies with the jam using a teaspoon. If the holes are not completely filled, scoop any remaining jam into a paper cone (see page 12) and pipe it in the gaps. These cookies are good for about four weeks stored in an airtight container at room temperature.

> **BAKING TIP:** Brush off any excess flour on the ring-shaped cookies to make sure the frosting will stick to the dough.

> **BAKING TIP:** Piping dots with the frosting on the unbaked rings will make the cookies look like white flowers.

Chocolate Flowers

These are one of the first cookies I ever made and one of my favorites. The dough tends to be a bit sticky depending on how fine the walnuts are milled, so add a little bit more flour to the dough as necessary. If you have time, roast the walnuts before you grind them. The roasting intensifies the flavor of the nut and makes the cookie tastier. The decoration is a bit time consuming, so if you are in a rush simply dip a spoon into the melted chocolate and drip fine lines on the flowers and then sprinkle them with almond sticks or chopped almonds. For this recipe you will need a flower-shaped cookie cutter that is about 1½ inches (4 cm) in diameter.

MAKES ABOUT 1½ DOZEN COOKIES

COOKIE DOUGH
¾ CUP (100 GRAMS) GROUND WALNUTS

1¼ CUPS (150 GRAMS) ALL-PURPOSE FLOUR

1 TEASPOON GRATED LEMON ZEST

1 MEDIUM EGG

⅔ CUP (125 GRAMS) GRANULATED SUGAR

1 TABLESPOON VANILLA SUGAR (SEE PAGE 14)

1⅛ STICKS (125 GRAMS) UNSALTED BUTTER, AT ROOM TEMPERATURE

FILLING
⅓ CUP (50 GRAMS) SEMISWEET CHOCOLATE CHIPS

7 OUNCES (200 GRAMS) CHOCOLATE NOUGAT

DECORATION
1 CUP (150 GRAMS) SEMISWEET CHOCOLATE

⅓ CUP (50 GRAMS) CHOPPED NUTS OR SLICED ALMONDS

1. **FOR THE COOKIE DOUGH:** Combine the dough ingredients in a bowl and, using the dough hook attachment of an electric mixer, knead until the dough is smooth, 3 to 5 minutes. Form the dough into a small loaf. Wrap the loaf in plastic wrap and let it rest in the refrigerator for about 60 minutes.

2. Preheat the oven to 350°F (175°C).

3. Lightly flour a working surface and roll the dough out thinly, about ⅛ inch (3 mm) thick. Using the flower cookie cutter cut the dough into 36 cookies.

4. Line a baking sheet with parchment paper and then transfer the flowers carefully to the sheet with a pastry spatula. Bake the cookies for 13 minutes or until lightly golden. Carefully remove them from the baking sheet with the pastry spatula and place them on a cooling rack to cool completely.

5. **FOR THE FILLING:** Melt the chocolate (see page 10). Add the nougat to the warm chocolate and stir well until the nougat is melted. Spread one or two teaspoons of the filling on a baked cookie and cover it with a second cookie. Repeat with the remaining cookies and filling.

6. FOR THE DECORATION: Melt the chocolate (see page 10) and scoop it into a paper cone. Using the cone, decorate the edges or tops of the cookies with the chocolate. Press chopped nuts or almond slices into the chocolate on the cookies to resemble petals. These cookies are good for about five weeks stored in an air-tight container at room temperature.

> **BAKING TIP:** If you can't find chocolate nougat, you can substitute peanut butter cups to add an interesting flavor twist.

Chocolate Sandwich

This cookie is for chocolate-devoted people. Because of their manufacturing techniques and high quality ingredients, Belgian chocolates are quite distinctive and are considered the gold standard for chocolates throughout the world. I created this recipe based on Belgian chocolate; it transforms a simple chocolate cookie into a delicious multi-faceted treat. For this recipe you will need a round cookie cutter that is about $1\frac{1}{3}$ inches (3 cm) in diameter.

MAKES ABOUT 3 DOZEN COOKIES

COOKIE DOUGH

$2\frac{1}{2}$ CUPS (300 GRAMS) ALL-PURPOSE FLOUR

$\frac{3}{4}$ CUP (80 GRAMS) GROUND HAZELNUTS

$1\frac{1}{3}$ CUPS (160 GRAMS) CONFECTIONERS' SUGAR

2 STICKS (200 GRAMS) UNSALTED BUTTER, AT ROOM TEMPERATURE

PINCH OF SALT

1 MEDIUM EGG

FILLING

2 TABLESPOONS CONFECTIONERS' SUGAR

7 TABLESPOONS (100 MILLILITERS) HEAVY CREAM

$\frac{2}{3}$ CUP (100 GRAMS) SEMISWEET CHOCOLATE CHIPS

$3\frac{1}{2}$ OUNCES (100 GRAMS) CHOCOLATE NOUGAT OR HAZELNUT SPREAD

DECORATION

$1\frac{1}{4}$ CUPS (200 GRAMS) SEMISWEET CHOCOLATE

$\frac{1}{3}$ CUP (50 GRAMS) CHOPPED PISTACHIO NUTS OR CHOCOLATE SHAVINGS

1. **FOR THE COOKIE DOUGH:** Combine the dough ingredients in a bowl and, using the dough hook attachment of an electric mixer, knead until the dough is smooth, 3 to 5 minutes. Form the dough into a small loaf. Wrap the loaf in plastic wrap and let it rest in the refrigerator for about 30 to 45 minutes.

2. Preheat the oven to 350°F (175°C).

3. Lightly flour a working surface and roll the dough out thinly, about $\frac{1}{8}$ inch (3 mm) thick. Using the round cookie cutter cut the dough into small circles.

4. Line a baking sheet with parchment paper and then transfer the cookies carefully to the sheet with a pastry spatula. Bake the cookies for about 10 minutes or until lightly golden. Be sure to not let them turn brown. Carefully remove them from the baking sheet with the pastry spatula and place them on a cooling rack to cool completely.

5. **FOR THE FILLING:** Heat the confectioners' sugar in a pan over medium heat until it caramelizes. Pour in the cream and stir with a spoon until the sugar is dissolved. Remove the pan from the stove and

stir in the semisweet chocolate and the nougat. Allow the cream to cool to lukewarm.

6. Pour the cream into a paper cone (see page 12) or use a teaspoon and spread it on half of the cookies. Cover the filling with the remaining cookies to make 36 sandwiches.

7. **FOR THE DECORATION:** Melt the semisweet chocolate (see page 10) and use a teaspoon to spread it on top of the filled cookies. Sprinkle each cookie with pistachio nuts or chocolate shavings. Return the cookies to the cooling rack to cool at room temperature until the chocolate is firm. These cookies are good for about one week stored in an airtight container at room temperature.

BAKING TIP: Ground hazelnuts are great in the cookie dough, but if you have more time and want to intensify the flavor, roast whole hazelnuts in the oven (350°F/176°C for 15 minutes) and let them cool. Put them into a plastic bag, close it, and rub the bag with your hands to remove the skins. Grind the nuts in a mixer.

Chocolate Wedges

This dessert is basically a Baumkuchen ("Tree Cake") cut into wedges and covered with chocolate. Baumkuchen is a type of layered cake served as a traditional dessert in many European countries. Surprisingly, it is also a popular snack in Japan, especially for weddings. It usually is baked on a spit by brushing on even layers of batter and then rotating the thick metal rod around the heat source. When the cake is removed and sliced, it has a hole in the middle. Each layer is divided from the next by a strip of brown dough resembling growth rings on a crosscut tree, hence the name, "Tree Cake". Contrary to popular belief, the Hungarian and Transylvanian (Romanian) version of this cake, Kürtöskalács, is not connected with the Tree Cake. The only thing they have in common is that they are both baked on a spit and are both equally delicious.

MAKES ABOUT 3 DOZEN PIECES

DOUGH
$2^1/_4$ STICKS (260 GRAMS) UNSALTED BUTTER, AT ROOM TEMPERATURE

$^3/_4$ CUP (180 GRAMS) GRANULATED SUGAR

GRATED ZEST OF 1 LEMON

5 MEDIUM EGGS

1 CUP (125 GRAMS) ALL-PURPOSE FLOUR

1 CUP (125 GRAMS) CORNSTARCH

$^2/_3$ CUP (100 GRAMS) GROUND ALMONDS

1 TABLESPOON ROSE WATER OR ORANGE JUICE

$^1/_2$ TEASPOON GROUND CINNAMON

1 TABLESPOON RUM

FILLING
4 TABLESPOONS APRICOT JAM

DECORATION
$2^1/_2$ CUPS (300 GRAMS) MILK OR SEMISWEET CHOCOLATE CHIPS

1. Preheat the oven to about 475°F (250°C).
2. **FOR THE COOKIE DOUGH:** Combine the dough ingredients in the bowl of an electric mixer knead the dough until smooth, 3 to 5 minutes.
3. Line a small rectangle baking pan ($7^3/_4$ x 12 inches or 20 x 30 cm) with parchment paper and spread a thin layer of the dough ($^1/_8$ inch or 3 mm) on the bottom of the pan. Bake the layer of dough for 2 minutes.
4. Remove the dough from the oven. Immediately spread another thin layer over the baked layer. Bake the two layers for 1 to 2 minutes. Continue this step until all of the dough is used.
5. Remove the pan from the oven and set it on a cooling rack. Let it stand for about 10 minutes and then take

a spatula or knife and run it around the edge of the cake to loosen it from the sides of the baking pan. Place a wire cooling rack on top of the cake and baking pan and flip it so the wire rack is on the bottom. Let it cool and then cut the cake in half crosswise.

6. **FOR THE FILLING:** Heat the jam in the microwave or in a small pot on the stovetop until it is pourable and then spread it onto the top of the halved cake and place the other half on top. Let it rest for 20 minutes to allow the jam to seep into the dough and moisten it.

7. Use a sharp knife to cut about 18 squares from the loaf and then cut each of them into small triangles. Put the triangles on an oiled cooling rack.

8. **FOR THE DECORATION:** Melt the chocolate (see page 10). Pour the melted chocolate over the wedges while they are on the cooling rack, or use a bowl and dip the wedges into the chocolate. Let the chocolate-covered wedges rest on the cooling rack until the chocolate dries completely. These cookies are good for about four weeks stored in an airtight container at room temperature.

BAKING TIP: If you oil the cooling rack before placing the wedges on it, the chocolate will not stick and it will be easier to remove them when the chocolate dries.

BAKING TIP: The wedges may seem dry but the dough stays moist and should have a fluffy texture.

Coconut Swirls

This delicious cookie combines the sweetness of coconut flakes with the chocolate flavor of cocoa. Cocoa may have originated in South America, but it was first cultivated in Central America in 1500 BC. Chocolate with a high cocoa and cacao percentage may contain beneficial cardiovascular effects due to their high level of flavonoids, also known as vitamin P.

MAKES ABOUT 6 DOZEN COOKIES

COOKIE DOUGH

1¾ CUPS (220 GRAMS) ALL-PURPOSE FLOUR

¼ CUP (25 GRAMS) SEMISWEET COCOA POWDER

¾ CUP (150 GRAMS) GRANULATED SUGAR

1 MEDIUM EGG

1 STICK (115 GRAMS) UNSALTED BUTTER, AT ROOM TEMPERATURE

1 TABLESPOON MILK

½ TEASPOON BAKING POWDER

FILLING

½ CUP (100 GRAMS) CREAM CHEESE

⅓ CUP (80 GRAMS) GRANULATED SUGAR

2 TABLESPOONS VANILLA SUGAR (SEE PAGE 14)

½ STICK (55 GRAMS) BUTTER, AT ROOM TEMPERATURE

GRATED ZEST OF 1 ORANGE

1 CUP (75 GRAMS) UNSWEETENED COCONUT FLAKES

⅓ CUP (50 GRAMS) GROUND HAZELNUTS

1. **FOR THE COOKIE DOUGH:** Combine the dough ingredients in a bowl and, using the dough hook attachment of an electric mixer, knead until the dough is smooth, 3 to 5 minutes. Form the dough into a small loaf. Wrap the loaf in plastic wrap and let it rest in the refrigerator for about 30 minutes.

2. **FOR THE FILLING:** In a bowl mix together the cream cheese, granulated sugar, vanilla sugar, butter, orange zest, coconut flakes, and hazelnuts. Put the filling in the refrigerator while preparing the dough.

3. On a lightly floured working surface, roll the dough out between two pieces of plastic wrap until it is about ⅛ inch (3 mm) thick and resembles an 8 x 11-inch (20 x 30 cm) rectangle.

4. Remove the filling from the refrigerator and spread it evenly on the dough. Starting at the longer side of the rectangle, roll it to create a swirling pattern of filling at the end of the log. Wrap the log in plastic wrap and place it in the refrigerator for 3 hours or overnight.

5. Preheat the oven to about 375°F (190°C).

6. Use a sharp knife and cut the roll into ¼-inch (5-mm) slices. Line a baking sheet with parchment paper and gently transfer the cookies to the sheet with a pastry spatula. Bake the cookies for 10 minutes. Carefully remove them from the baking sheet with the pastry spatula and place them on a cooling rack to cool completely. These cookies are good for about three weeks stored in an airtight container at room temperature.

BAKING TIP: For a different, delicious flavor, substitute chopped hazelnuts for the coconut.

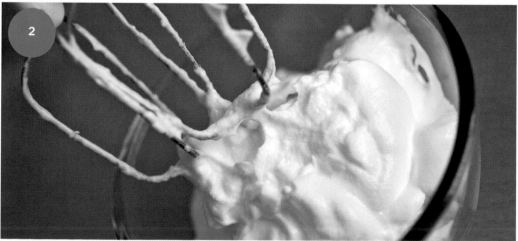

Coffee Shots

Italians did not invent the coffee drink, but our present coffee culture did originate in Italy. The first European coffee house was opened in Venice in 1645 and its popularity spread quickly. Italy became the stronghold of coffee drinks and every Italian enjoyed coffee with their breakfast. This cookie is dominated by the overwhelming taste and color of coffee, so I only recommend it to true coffee lovers or those with some Italian ancestry. For this recipe you will need a round cookie cutter that is about 1½ inches (4 cm) in diameter.

MAKES ABOUT 3 DOZEN COOKIES

COOKIE DOUGH

1¼ STICKS (145 GRAMS) UNSALTED BUTTER, AT ROOM TEMPERATURE

⅔ CUP (70 GRAMS) CONFECTIONERS' SUGAR

1 MEDIUM EGG YOLK

½ CUP (70 GRAMS) GROUND ALMONDS

1⅔ CUPS (200 GRAMS) ALL-PURPOSE FLOUR

FILLING

1 CUP (100 GRAMS) CONFECTIONERS' SUGAR

¾ STICK (85 GRAMS) UNSALTED BUTTER, AT ROOM TEMPERATURE

1½ TEASPOONS INSTANT COFFEE

DECORATION

1 CUP (100 GRAMS) CONFECTIONERS' SUGAR

1 TEASPOON INSTANT COFFEE

2 TABLESPOONS COLD BREWED COFFEE

COFFEE CHOCOLATE DROPS OR CHOCOLATE-COVERED ESPRESSO BEANS

1. **FOR THE COOKIE DOUGH:** Combine the butter and confectioners' sugar in the bowl of an electric mixer fitted with the paddle attachment and beat until the mixture resembles a smooth paste, 3 to 5 minutes. Add the egg yolk, ground almonds, and flour, switch the electric mixer to the dough hook attachment, and mix until the dough is smooth, 3 to 5 minutes. Form the dough into a small loaf. Wrap the loaf in plastic wrap and put it in the refrigerator for about 30 minutes.

2. Preheat the oven to 350°F (180°C).

3. Lightly flour a working surface and roll the dough to about ⅛ inch (3 mm) thick. Using the round cookie cut the dough into 72 cookies.

4. Line a baking sheet with parchment paper and then transfer the cookies carefully to the sheet with a pastry spatula. Bake the cookies for 7 to 10 minutes or until the edges turn golden brown. Carefully remove them from the baking sheet with the pastry spatula and place them on a cooling rack to cool completely.

5. **FOR THE FILLING:** Stir the confectioners' sugar, butter, and instant coffee together in a medium bowl with a fork until it resembles a smooth paste. Using a spoon spread a teaspoon of filling on half of the cookies and then top them with the remaining cookies.

6. **FOR THE DECORATION:** Mix the confectioners' sugar and the instant coffee into the brewed coffee in a medium bowl until they are dissolved. Spread the mixture on top of the filled cookies with a teaspoon and decorate each cookie with a chocolate drop or espresso bean. These cookies are good for about one week stored in an airtight container at room temperature.

Walnut Bites

This filled cookie is very moist and has a very intense citrus flavor thanks to orange marmalade, a preserve made from citrus fruits boiled with sugar and water and usually with the rind of the fruit. In this recipe you can use whatever variation you want of orange preserve, so if you don't like the slightly bitter taste of the marmalade, just use apricot jam. It will taste different and will be a bit sweeter, but in my experience, kids prefer the apricot flavor. For this recipe you will need a round cookie cutter that is about 2 inches (5 cm) in diameter.

MAKES ABOUT 2 DOZEN COOKIES

COOKIE DOUGH

2 CUPS (250 GRAMS) ALL-PURPOSE FLOUR

$1/4$ CUP (40 GRAMS) GRANULATED SUGAR

2 TABLESPOONS VANILLA SUGAR (SEE PAGE 14)

PINCH OF SALT

$2/3$ CUP (150 GRAMS) SOUR CREAM

1 STICK (113 GRAMS) UNSALTED BUTTER, AT ROOM TEMPERATURE

FILLING

$3^1/2$ OUNCES (100 GRAMS) MARZIPAN

$2/3$ CUP (100 GRAMS) CHOPPED NUTS

$1/3$ CUP (100 GRAMS) ORANGE MARMALADE OR APRICOT JAM

1 MEDIUM EGG WHITE

DECORATION

1 MEDIUM EGG YOLK

3 TABLESPOONS MILK

$1/2$ CUP (50 GRAMS) CHOPPED OR SLICED ALMONDS

1. **FOR THE COOKIE DOUGH:** Combine the dough ingredients in a bowl and, using the dough hook attachment of an electric mixer, knead until the dough is smooth, 3 to 5 minutes. Form the dough into a small loaf. Wrap the loaf in plastic wrap and let it rest in the refrigerator for about 30 minutes.

2. **FOR THE FILLING:** Grate the marzipan into a small bowl, add the nuts and jam, and stir thoroughly with a fork.

3. Preheat the oven to 375°F (190°C).

4. Lightly flour a working surface and roll the dough out thinly, about $1/8$ inch (3 mm) thick. Using the round cookie cutter cut the dough into 72 cookies.

5. Line a baking sheet with parchment paper and then transfer the cookies carefully to the sheet with a pastry spatula. Whisk the egg white in a small bowl and brush it on half of the cookies. Fill those cookies

with 1 teaspoon of the marzipan filling and then top with the remaining cookies. Flatten the cookies slightly and press the edges down with a fork to close the sandwiches.

6. **FOR THE DECORATION:** Whisk the egg yolk with the milk and brush the mixture on top of the filled cookies. Place six or so almond slices on top of each cookie. Bake the cookies for 15 minutes or until lightly golden. Carefully remove them from the baking sheet with the pastry spatula and place them on a cooling rack to cool completely. These cookies are good for two weeks stored in an airtight container at room temperature.

Flaming Hearts

One of my favorite cookies is Flaming Hearts. It takes a lot of work to make them, but you will be rewarded with gratitude and amazement. The cookies taste refreshing and crunchy because of the lemon icing, but they are not sour. Wrapped in cellophane bags or enclosed in a nice box, they make a perfect gift for a beloved person and they are perfect for a romantic occasion. I once baked Flaming Hearts for a wedding and they were a tremendous success. For this recipe you will need a heart-shaped cookie cutter that is about 1 inch (3 cm) in diameter.

MAKES ABOUT 3 DOZEN COOKIES

COOKIE DOUGH

2 CUPS (250 GRAMS) ALL-PURPOSE FLOUR

$1^1/_2$ STICKS (150 GRAMS) UNSALTED BUTTER, AT ROOM TEMPERATURE

$^2/_3$ CUP (70 GRAMS) CONFECTIONERS' SUGAR

2 MEDIUM EGG YOLKS

GRATED ZEST OF 1 LEMON

FILLING

$^1/_2$ CUP (140 GRAMS) STRAWBERRY JAM

DECORATION

4 TABLESPOONS RED SEEDLESS JAM OR JELLY

1 CUP (100 GRAMS) CONFECTIONERS' SUGAR

3 TABLESPOONS LEMON JUICE

1. **FOR THE COOKIE DOUGH:** Combine the dough ingredients in a bowl and, using the dough hook attachment of an electric mixer, knead until the dough is smooth, 3 to 5 minutes. Form the dough into a small loaf. Wrap the loaf in plastic wrap and let it rest in the refrigerator for about 30 minutes.

2. Preheat the oven to 350°F (175°C).

3. Lightly flour a working surface and roll the dough out thinly, about $^1/_8$ inch (3 mm) thick. Using the heart-shaped cookie cutter cut the dough into 72 cookies.

4. Line a baking sheet with parchment paper and then transfer the cookies carefully to the sheet with a pastry spatula. Bake the cookies in the oven for 15 minutes. Be sure to not let them turn brown. Carefully remove them from the baking sheet with the pastry spatula and place them on a cooling rack to cool completely.

5. **FOR THE FILLING:** Remove the cooled cookies from the rack and spread $^1/_2$ teaspoon of strawberry jam on half of the cookies. Place the remaining cookies on top of the jam to form sandwiches.

6. **FOR THE DECORATION:** Melt the seedless jam or jelly in a small pot over low heat until it becomes

fluid. In a small bowl, mix together the confectioner's sugar and the lemon juice until the mixture is creamy. Spread the sugar-lemon mixture on top of the filled cookies using a toothpick or a small teaspoon.

7. Dip a toothpick in the red jam or jelly and make two thin lines on the white topping. Use the toothpick to spread the jam to create little "flames." Let the cookies dry on a cooling rack. These cookies are good for four weeks.

BAKING TIP: Decorating each cookie takes about 1 minute, and they all should be done all at one time because the sugar topping will get too hard to draw the "flames" if you let it dry.

BAKING TIP: Add 2 to 3 drops of red food coloring to the jam to make the "flames" more vibrant.

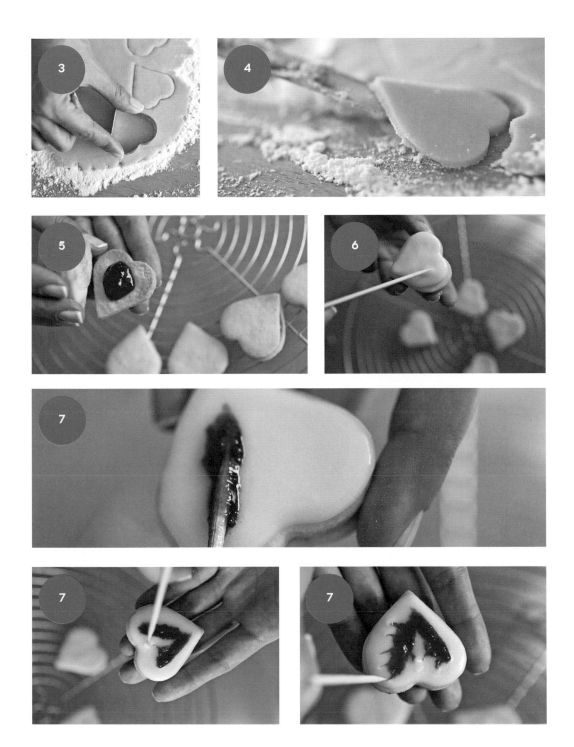

Walnut Flowers

Walnuts are native to the mountain ranges of Central Asia. Greeks proclaim that they brought the tree to Europe around the seventh to fifth century BC. Today, this nut is known as a delicacy and is incorporated into desserts and pralines all over Europe and Asia. Walnuts contain a high percentage of omega-3 fatty acids, which is very beneficial for the function of the brain and heart. In addition, they contain many vitamins, including vitamin E and zinc, which are essential for liver function and healthy skin and hair. For this recipe you will need one fluted round or flower-shaped cookie cutter that is about 1½ inches (4 cm) in diameter.

MAKES ABOUT 2 DOZEN COOKIES

COOKIE DOUGH
¾ CUP (100 GRAMS) GROUND WALNUTS

1⅔ CUPS (200 GRAMS) ALL-PURPOSE FLOUR

⅔ CUP (150 GRAMS) GRANULATED SUGAR

1 VANILLA BEAN OR 1 TABLESPOON VANILLA SUGAR (SEE PAGE 14)

2 STICKS (200 GRAMS) UNSALTED BUTTER, AT ROOM TEMPERATURE

FILLING
6 TABLESPOONS RED CURRENT JAM

DECORATION
2 CUPS (200 GRAMS) CONFECTIONERS' SUGAR

2 TO 3 TABLESPOONS LEMON JUICE

42 WALNUT HALVES

1. **FOR THE COOKIE DOUGH:** Combine the dough ingredients in a bowl and, using the dough hook attachment of an electric mixer, knead until the dough is smooth, 3 to 5 minutes. Form the dough into a small loaf. Wrap the loaf in plastic wrap and let it rest in the refrigerator for about 60 minutes.

2. Preheat the oven to about 350°F (180°C).

3. Lightly flour a working surface and roll the dough out thinly, about ⅛ inch (3 mm) thick. Using the fluted round or flower-shaped cookie cutter cut the dough into about 84 cookies.

4. Line a baking sheet with parchment paper and then transfer the cookies carefully to the sheet with a pastry spatula. Bake the cookies for 10 to 13 minutes or until lightly golden. Be sure to not let them turn brown. Carefully remove them from the baking sheet with the pastry spatula and place them on a cooling rack to cool completely.

5. **FOR THE FILLING:** Heat the jam in the microwave or in a pot over the stovetop until it is pourable. Spread the warm jam on half of the cookies and then top the jam with the remaining cookies, making 42 sandwich cookies.

6. FOR THE DECORATION: Mix the confectioner's sugar with the lemon juice in a small bowl and then scoop the mixture into a paper cone (see page 12). Using the cone, draw grids with the mixture on each cookie; press a walnut half into the center of each cookie. Let the decorated cookies dry completely on the cooling rack. These cookies are good for about three weeks stored in an airtight container at room temperature.

BAKING TIP: When creating the grid decoration, you can also use melted white chocolate instead of the confectioners' sugar. The white chocolate will look more vibrant and the cookie will taste sweeter.

BAKING TIP: Using ground walnuts saves you time, but if time is not an issue, then try roasting whole walnuts and grinding them yourself for a more intense flavor. Roast whole walnuts in a single layer on a baking sheet for about 8 minutes in a 375°F (190°C) oven or you can roast them in a dry frying pan over medium heat for 5 minutes, stirring frequently. Allow them to cool off. Next, put them into a clean plastic bag, close it, and rub them between your hands—the skin will come right off. Take the semi-skinless walnuts out of the bag and grind them in a food processor.

Jam Blossoms

This is a modified recipe of the Hearts and Stars Linzer Cookies (see page 80). One of my fixations, as a cook, is to make tiny, one-bite treats. Most cookies and confections look more appealing when they are made smaller than the original. When something is made bite-size, you can taste the flavors of all the ingredients simultaneously.

One day, I bought a tiny flower cookie cutter and experimented with the Linzer dough. The result was a cute little flower with a fruity taste that instantly melts in your mouth. It was a great success and my family and friends loved it. The only thing they complained about is that I didn't make enough cookies! These cookies may take a bit more time and patience to make due to the fragile dough and their tiny size, but the results more than justify the effort. For this recipe you will need one flower-shaped cookie cutter that is about $1\frac{1}{4}$ inches (3 cm) in diameter.

MAKES ABOUT 4 DOZEN COOKIES

COOKIE DOUGH

$2\frac{1}{2}$ CUPS (300 GRAMS) ALL-PURPOSE FLOUR

1 CUP (120 GRAMS) CONFECTIONERS' SUGAR

1 TABLESPOON VANILLA SUGAR (SEE PAGE 14)

$1\frac{1}{2}$ STICKS (150 GRAMS) UNSALTED BUTTER, AT ROOM TEMPERATURE

1 MEDIUM EGG

FILLING

$\frac{1}{4}$ CUP (60 GRAMS) APRICOT JAM

1 TABLESPOON DRY WHITE WINE

DECORATION

5 TABLESPOONS CONFECTIONERS' SUGAR

1. **FOR THE COOKIE DOUGH:** Combine the dough ingredients in a bowl and, using the dough hook attachment of an electric mixer, knead until the dough is smooth, 3 to 5 minutes. Form the dough into a small loaf. Wrap the loaf in plastic wrap and let it rest in the refrigerator for about 30 minutes.

2. Preheat the oven to 350°F (175°C).

3. Lightly flour a working surface and roll the dough out thinly, about $\frac{1}{8}$ inch (3 mm) thick. Using the small flower-shaped cookie cutter cut the dough into about 96 cookies. Use a small tube or straw to cut out the centers of half of the cookies, and use a toothpick to remove the dough from the centers of the cut-out flowers.

4. Line a baking sheet with parchment paper and then transfer the flowers carefully to the sheet with a pastry spatula. Bake the cookies for 10 minutes, until lightly golden. Be sure to not let them turn brown. Carefully remove them from the baking sheet with the pastry spatula and place them on a cooling rack to cool completely.

5. **FOR THE FILLING:** Heat the jam in the microwave or in a pot over a stovetop until it is pourable. Add

the wine and stir well to combine. Use a spoon to spread the jam mixture onto the solid cookies and then place the cut-out cookies on top. If the holes are not completely filled with jam, scoop any remaining jam into a paper cone (see page 12) and fill in the gaps.

6. **FOR THE DECORATION:** Sprinkle the tops of the cookies with confectioners' sugar. These cookies are good for about three weeks stored in an airtight container at room temperature.

Pineapple Peaks

The ingredient that makes this cookie so special is the dried pineapple. Dried fruit has had the majority of the water removed either by drying in the sun or putting the slices in specialized dryers or food dehydrators. Dried papayas and pineapples actually count as candied fruits, since they are preserved by being cooked in sugar syrup, which absorbs their moisture. This particular form of food preservation was common in ancient Chinese and Roman cultures. Since the sixteenth century, dried fruits of many kinds became important to the cuisines of countries throughout the world.

MAKES ABOUT THREE DOZEN COOKIES

COOKIE DOUGH

7 OUNCES (200 GRAMS) MARZIPAN

1 MEDIUM EGG YOLK

1/2 STICK (55 GRAMS) UNSALTED BUTTER, AT ROOM TEMPERATURE

2/3 CUP (100 GRAMS) GROUND ALMONDS

3 TABLESPOONS ALL–PURPOSE FLOUR

FILLING

ABOUT 40 PIECES OF DRIED PINEAPPLE

DECORATION

1 MEDIUM EGG WHITE

2/3 CUP (100 GRAMS) CHOPPED ALMONDS

1. Preheat the oven to 400°F (200°C).

2. FOR THE COOKIE DOUGH: Grate the marzipan into a bowl. Add the egg yolk and butter and mix well with a hand mixer or a spoon. Add the almonds and flour and, using the dough hook attachment of an electric mixer, knead until the dough is smooth, 3 to 5 minutes. Form the dough into a small loaf. Wrap the loaf in plastic wrap and let it rest in the refrigerator for about 30 minutes.

3. FOR THE FILLING: Using a sharp knife, chop the dried pineapple into small (about 1/4-inch or 6-mm) pieces.

4. Lightly flour a working surface and use your hands to roll the dough into a long log. Using a sharp knife cut the dough into 40 pieces. Form each piece of the dough into little balls and flatten them. Place a piece of the pineapple in the middle of each cookie. Shape the cookies into little cones.

5. FOR THE DECORATION: Whisk the egg white in a small bowl, and place the chopped almonds in a shallow dish. Use a pastry brush to spread the egg white on the lower edge of the cones and then roll the edges of the cookies in the chopped almonds.

6. Line a baking sheet with parchment paper and then transfer the cones carefully to the pan with a pastry spatula. Bake the cookies for 10 to 13 minutes or until lightly golden. Be sure to not let them turn brown. Carefully remove them from the baking sheet with the pastry spatula and place them on a cooling rack to cool completely. These cookies are good for about five weeks stored in an airtight container at room temperature.

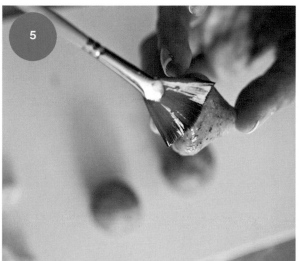

Ruby Eyes

This recipe is inspired by antique gold animal brooches that are decorated with all different types of gemstones. The animal's eyes are often red—some rubies and some glass. My cookie version of these glittery accessories looks like a golden brooch with small diamonds on the edge and a big ruby in the middle, and some people call it edible jewelry. The only thing missing is the metal pin on the back. For this recipe you will need one round cookie cutter that is about 1½ inch (4 cm) in diameter.

MAKES ABOUT 3 DOZEN COOKIES

COOKIE DOUGH

3 CUPS (350 GRAMS) ALL-PURPOSE FLOUR

1⅛ CUPS (125 GRAMS) CONFECTIONERS' SUGAR

1 TABLESPOON VANILLA SUGAR (SEE PAGE 14)

1½ STICKS (170 GRAMS) UNSALTED BUTTER, AT ROOM TEMPERATURE

2 MEDIUM EGG YOLKS

2 TABLESPOONS MILK

GRATED ZEST OF ½ LEMON

FILLING

½ CUP (120 MILLILITERS) MILK

⅔ CUP (130 GRAMS) GRANULATED SUGAR

½ TEASPOON GROUND CINNAMON

GRATED ZEST OF ½ LEMON

2 CUPS (240 GRAMS) GROUND WALNUTS

4 TABLESPOONS VANILLA SUGAR (SEE PAGE 14)

3 TABLESPOONS RUM OR ORANGE JUICE

DECORATION

⅔ CUP (50 GRAMS) UNSWEETENED COCONUT FLAKES

¼ CUP (70 GRAMS) APRICOT JAM

½ CUP (140 GRAMS) STRAWBERRY JAM

1. FOR THE COOKIE DOUGH: Combine the dough ingredients in a bowl and, using the dough hook attachment of an electric mixer, knead until the dough is smooth, 3 to 5 minutes. Form the dough into a small loaf. Wrap the loaf in plastic wrap and let it rest in the refrigerator for about 30 minutes.

2. Preheat the oven to 350°F (175°C).

3. Lightly flour a working surface and roll the dough out thinly, about ⅛ inch (3 mm) thick. Use the round cookie cutter to cut the dough into about 72 circles.

4. Line a baking sheet with parchment paper and then transfer the cookies carefully to the sheet with a pastry spatula. Bake for 10 to 13 minutes until they are golden brown. Be sure to not let them turn brown. Carefully remove them from the baking sheet with the pastry spatula and place them on a cooling rack to cool completely.

5. FOR THE FILLING: Warm the milk in a medium saucepan over medium heat and then add the remaining filling ingredients and stir to combine. Cook it for 3 to 5 minutes or until it thickens to a paste-like consistency. Remove the pan from the heat and allow the mixture to cool. Scoop the filling into a paper cone (page 12) or use a teaspoon to spread the filling generously on half of the cookies. Top with the remaining cookies.

6. FOR THE DECORATION: Sprinkle the coconut flakes onto a flat plate. Heat the apricot and strawberry jams separately in the microwave or in a pot over a stovetop until they are pourable. Use a brush to spread the warm apricot jam around the edges of the cookies and then roll them in the coconut flakes. Finally, pipe a dab of the warm strawberry jam in the middle of each cookie for a lovely center. Let the cookies dry completely on the cooling rack. These cookies are good for about one week stored in an airtight container at room temperature.

BAKING TIP: Once the cookies are done be sure not to stack them on top of each other. Otherwise, the jam will make them stick together.

Strawberry Rolls

My little brother, whose favorite color is red, requested that I create this cookie for him. After listening to his specifications for the perfect cookie, this was the resulting recipe. The cookie is based on a simple dough with a rich red color and intense strawberry flavor.

Rumor has it that red food coloring is made from beetles. And indeed, it is true that common red food colorants (cochineal and carmine) are made from ground up dried Central and South American beetles. These species of beetles live deep within cacti plants and were used as a red dye for centuries by the Aztecs, Mayans, and Native Americans. Aside from being used in food products, dyes made from these beetles are also used in paint, cosmetics, shampoos, and even in some fruit juices. But there are other red food dyes that have nothing to do with beetles. So don't worry, just read the ingredient list. But be careful, other dyes are usually made from petroleum or coal tar products, which may be unhealthy.

MAKES ABOUT 4 DOZEN COOKIES

COOKIE DOUGH
2 CUPS (250 GRAMS) ALL-PURPOSE FLOUR

$1\frac{1}{2}$ STICKS (150 GRAMS) UNSALTED BUTTER, AT ROOM TEMPERATURE

$\frac{2}{3}$ CUP (70 GRAMS) CONFECTIONERS' SUGAR

2 MEDIUM EGG YOLKS

FILLING
1 TABLESPOON STRAWBERRY JAM

3 DROPS RED FOOD COLORING

2 TABLESPOONS ALL-PURPOSE FLOUR

ADDITIONAL INGREDIENTS
1 MEDIUM EGG WHITE

1. **FOR THE COOKIE DOUGH:** Combine the dough ingredients in a bowl and, using the dough hook attachment of an electric mixer, knead until the dough is smooth, 3 to 5 minutes. Form the dough into a small loaf. Wrap the loaf in plastic wrap and let it rest in the refrigerator for about 30 minutes.

2. **FOR THE FILLING:** Lightly flour a working surface. Cut $\frac{1}{3}$ of the dough from the loaf and mix in the jam, food coloring, and flour with your hands. If it is too sticky to work with, then add another tablespoon of flour. Using your hands, roll the red dough into a long log, about $\frac{2}{3}$ inch (2 cm) in diameter. Wrap the log in plastic wrap and put it in the freezer for 20 minutes. Be sure not to let the dough chill for longer than 20 minutes.

3. Lightly flour a working surface and roll the un-colored dough out thinly, about $\frac{1}{8}$ inch (3 mm) thick. Using a sharp knife cut out a rectangle that is the same length as the red dough log. In a small bowl whisk the egg white and use a pastry brush to spread it over the rectangle, reserving a tablespoon of the egg white.

4. Remove the red roll from the freezer and then place it horizontally in the center of the rectangle. Spread the remaining egg white on the red roll and wrap it with the un-colored dough. Wrap the red and white log in plastic wrap and put it in the freezer for another 20 minutes.

5. Preheat the oven to 350°F (180°C).

6. Line a baking sheet with parchment paper. Remove the log from the freezer and unwrap it on a floured surface. Using a sharp knife, slice the roll into thin slices about $^{1}/_{2}$ inch (1.3 cm) thick. Transfer the cookies carefully to the sheet with a pastry spatula. Bake the cookies for 13 minutes. Be sure to not let them turn brown. Carefully remove them from the baking sheet with the pastry spatula and place them on a cooling rack to cool completely. These cookies are good for about five weeks stored in an airtight container at room temperature.

Chapter 4

Challenging Cookies

Almond Mini Tartlet

The word tartlet (tartelette) is the diminutive form of the French word for tart. The custard tart, also known as doucette and dariole has existed since as early as the fourteenth century. French tarts are usually larger short crust pastries with a neutral taste, which means there is no salt or sugar added to the dough. Because the crust is neutral in taste, it can be filled with savory or sweet fillings. The most common tart fillings are custard and fruit. French pastry chefs fill mini tartlets with various fillings such as lemon, flan, chocolate, or in this case, almond cream. For this recipe you will need 36 mini tartlet molds and one round cookie cutter that is 2 inches (5 cm) in diameter.

MAKES ABOUT 3 DOZEN TARTLETS

TARTLET DOUGH
$1\frac{1}{3}$ STICKS (125 GRAMS) UNSALTED BUTTER, AT ROOM TEMPERATURE

1 CUP (100 GRAMS) CONFECTIONERS' SUGAR

PINCH OF SALT

2 SMALL EGG YOLKS

$1\frac{3}{4}$ CUPS (220 GRAMS) ALL-PURPOSE FLOUR

FILLING
5 TABLESPOONS (70 GRAMS) UNSALTED BUTTER, AT ROOM TEMPERATURE

GRATED ZEST OF $\frac{1}{2}$ LEMON

1 TEASPOON VANILLA SUGAR (SEE PAGE 14)

$\frac{1}{4}$ CUP (40 GRAMS) GRANULATED SUGAR

$\frac{2}{3}$ CUP (75 GRAMS) GROUND ALMONDS

1 MEDIUM EGG WHITE

$\frac{1}{3}$ CUP (40 GRAMS) ALL-PURPOSE FLOUR

DECORATION
3 TO 4 TABLESPOONS APRICOT JAM

18 CANDIED CHERRIES, HALVED

1. **FOR THE TARTLET DOUGH:** Combine the butter, confectioners' sugar, and egg yolks in a bowl and, using an electric mixer, beat until the mixture resembles a smooth paste, 3 to 5 minutes. Add the salt and flour and beat until the dough is smooth, 3 to 5 minutes. Form the dough into a small loaf. Wrap the loaf in plastic wrap and put it in the refrigerator for about 30 minutes.

2. **FOR THE FILLING:** Combine the butter, lemon zest, vanilla sugar, and granulated sugar in a bowl. Using the paddle attachment of an electric mixer beat until creamy, 3 to 5 minutes. In a small bowl, whisk together the ground almonds and the egg white and beat the mixture into the butter-sugar mixture. Slowly add the flour, beating until the mixture is creamy and smooth.

3. Place the filling into a piping bag fitted with a size 12 or 2A round piping tip.

4. Preheat the oven to 350 °F (180°C).

5. Butter 36 small tartlet molds. (If using silicone molds, you don't need to butter them.) Lightly flour a work surface and roll the dough out thinly, about $\frac{1}{8}$ inch (3 mm) thick. Using the 2-inch (5-cm) round cookie cutter cut the dough into 36 rounds and then press them into the molds, covering the bottom and sides. Place the molds on a baking sheet. Depending on the size of the oven, it may require the tart shells to be baked in two batches.

6. Pre-bake the tart shells for 7 minutes. Remove them from the oven, pipe the almond cream into the shells and then return them to the oven for an additional 12 minutes.

7. Transfer the baking sheet with the tartlets to a cooling rack and allow the tartlets to cool completely. When they are cool, carefully remove them from the molds and place them directly on the cooling rack.

8. FOR THE DECORATION: Heat the jam in the microwave or in a pot on the stovetop until it becomes pourable and then use a spoon to spread jam on each tartlet. Top each tartlet with one candied cherry half. These cookies are good for about two weeks stored in an airtight container at room temperature.

Black Sheep

The appearance of this cookie explains why it is named Black Sheep. It is not a fancy-looking biscuit at all, which makes it easily overlooked, but the flavor of the fruit inside the dough makes it unforgettable. If it's not the season for fresh berries, use plum or mixed berry jam instead.

MAKES ABOUT 4 DOZEN COOKIES

COOKIE DOUGH

2 CUPS (250 GRAMS) ALL-PURPOSE FLOUR

$1\frac{1}{4}$ STICKS (145 GRAMS) UNSALTED BUTTER, AT ROOM TEMPERATURE

$\frac{2}{3}$ CUP (70 GRAMS) CONFECTIONERS' SUGAR

2 MEDIUM EGG YOLKS

GRATED ZEST OF 1 LEMON

FILLING

$1\frac{2}{3}$ CUPS (250 GRAMS) FRESH BLUEBERRIES OR BLACKBERRIES OR JAM

DECORATION

CONFECTIONERS' SUGAR

1. **FOR THE COOKIE DOUGH:** Combine the dough ingredients in a bowl and, using the dough hook attachment of an electric mixer, knead until the dough is smooth, 3 to 5 minutes. Form the dough into a small disc. Wrap it in plastic wrap and let it rest in the refrigerator for about 30 minutes.

2. Lightly flour a work surface and roll the dough out thinly, about $\frac{1}{8}$ inch (3 mm) thick. Using a knife cut out two rectangles of the same size.

3. Preheat the oven to about 350°F (180°C).

4. **FOR THE FILLING:** Combine the berries or jam in a microwave-safe bowl and cook in the microwave for about 45 seconds on high heat until pourable. Alternatively, heat them in a small pot on the stovetop on medium heat for 1 to 2 minutes until they cook down to a pourable consistency. Spread the berries over each rectangle. Fold the rectangles in half lengthwise so that the jam is sandwiched in the middle. Seal the open edges of each rectangle with your finger so that the jam will not leak out as it bakes. Wrap them in plastic and place the two rectangles in the freezer for 20 minutes.

5. Line a baking sheet with parchment paper and place the semi-frozen dough on the sheet. Bake the two rectangles for 15 minutes or until lightly golden. Be sure to not let them turn brown. Carefully remove them from the baking sheet with a pastry spatula and place them on a cooling rack to cool completely.

6. **FOR THE DECORATION:** When the rectangles are cool, cut them into $\frac{1}{2}$-inch (1.3-cm) slices with a sharp knife and then sprinkle the top of the cookies with confectioners' sugar. These cookies are good for about five weeks stored in an airtight container at room temperature.

Cherry Kiss

Based on a French cookie called Boules d' Amandes or "almond ball," this little piece of heaven has a very intense flavor thanks to the marzipan, orange, and sour cherries, and it pairs deliciously with a hot drink of tea or strong unsweetened coffee. Although some recipes call for powdered almond, this one uses almond paste or marzipan.

MAKES ABOUT 1½ DOZEN COOKIES

COOKIE DOUGH
13 OUNCES (375 GRAMS) MARZIPAN

$^2/_3$ CUP (150 GRAMS) GRANULATED SUGAR

2 MEDIUM EGG WHITES

PINCH OF GROUND CINNAMON

GRATED ZEST OF $^1/_2$ LEMON

GRATED ZEST OF $^1/_2$ ORANGE

DECORATION
1$^1/_4$ CUPS (200 GRAMS) SLICED ALMONDS

FILLING
1$^1/_3$ CUPS (200 GRAMS) CANNED SOUR CHERRIES, WELL DRAINED

1. **FOR THE COOKIE DOUGH:** Grate the marzipan with the big holes on a box grater into a large bowl. Add the rest of the dough ingredients and, using an electric mixer, knead until the dough is smooth, 3 to 5 minutes. Spoon the dough into a paper or plastic cone (see page 12) fitted with a size 12 or 2A round piping tip.

2. Preheat the oven to 400°F (200°C).

3. **FOR THE DECORATION:** Pour the almond slices into shallow bowl or soup plate. Pipe out a strip of dough 1 inch (2.5 cm) long on top of the almonds.

4. **FOR THE FILLING:** Place a cherry in the middle of the dough strip and cover it by piping another strip of dough on top. Repeat the steps with the remaining dough and cherries

5. Sprinkle sliced almonds on top of each cookie and form it into a ball by pressing gently around the cherry.

6. Line a baking sheet with parchment paper and transfer the cookies to the sheet. Bake the cookies for 10 to 15 minutes or until lightly golden. Be sure to not let them turn brown. Carefully remove them from the baking sheet with a pastry spatula and place them on a cooling rack to cool completely. These cookies are good for about two weeks stored in an airtight container at room temperature.

BAKING TIP: Other nuts may be used instead of almonds, but remember that they have to be sliced.

Chessboard Cookies

This cookie belongs to the pastry family Teegebäck or "tea pastry", which comes from Germany. It is an exceptional looking biscuit and is usually served with tea or coffee. The great thing about this recipe is that you can color the yellow dough with any kind of food dye, and it will pick up the color beautifully. If you add a darker food dye instead of cocoa powder to the brown dough, you will have a different creation; let your imagination go wild.

MAKES ABOUT 12 DOZEN COOKIES

YELLOW DOUGH
1¾ STICKS (200 GRAMS) UNSALTED BUTTER, AT ROOM TEMPERATURE
2⅔ CUPS (300 GRAMS) ALL-PURPOSE FLOUR
1 CUP (100 GRAMS) CONFECTIONERS' SUGAR
2 MEDIUM EGG YOLKS

BROWN DOUGH
1¾ STICKS (200 GRAMS) UNSALTED BUTTER, AT ROOM TEMPERATURE
2⅔ CUPS (300 GRAMS) ALL-PURPOSE FLOUR
1 CUP (100 GRAMS) CONFECTIONERS' SUGAR
¾ CUP (80 GRAMS) COCOA POWDER
2 MEDIUM EGG YOLKS

ADDITIONAL INGREDIENTS
2 MEDIUM EGG WHITES, LIGHTLY BEATEN

1. Combine the ingredients for the yellow and brown doughs in two separate medium bowls. Mix both doughs with an electric mixer until smooth, 3 to 5 minutes. Form each dough into a small loaf and wrap each loaf in plastic wrap. Place the two loaves of dough in the refrigerator and let them rest for about 60 minutes.

2. Lightly flour a working surface and roll the yellow dough out thinly, about ¼-inch (6 mm) thickness. The easiest way to equally flatten the dough is to put it between two cutting boards of the same thickness. Divide the dough into four equal pieces.

3. Repeat step 2 with three quarters of the brown dough, and keep one quarter of the brown dough unrolled for step 5.

4. Cut 5 yellow and 4 brown strips of the dough of equal lengths. Place one yellow strip on the lightly floured working surface. Lightly spread beaten egg white on one side of the strip and place a brown strip next to the yellow strip and gently press so they stick to each other. Repeat the process with another yellow strip. Place a brown strip on top of the outside yellow strip and repeat the process alternating colored strips until you have a cube of three rows of alternating colored strips three wide and three high that form a chessboard pattern. Wrap the dough in foil and rest it in the refrigerator for about 30 minutes.

5. Remove the chessboard log from the refrigerator and brush it with the remaining egg whites. Roll out the remaining brown dough on a floured surface and place the chessboard on top of it. Wrap the chessboard carefully with the brown dough and put it back into the refrigerator for 1 hour.

6. Preheat the oven to 350°F (180°C).

7. Remove the dough from the refrigerator and cut it in $^{1}/_{4}$-inch (6-mm) slices. Line a baking sheet with parchment paper and then transfer the cookies carefully to the sheet with a pastry spatula. Bake the cookies for 15 minutes or until lightly golden. Carefully remove them from the baking sheet and allow them to cool completely on a cooling rack. These cookies are good for about five weeks stored in an airtight container at room temperature.

BAKING TIP: To mix it up you can switch the colors of the chessboard so that the outside cover dough is yellow instead of brown.

Chocolate Marzipan Sandwiches

The design of this cookie is usually used for chocolate candy. But, because of the very exquisite filling of marzipan and semisweet chocolate (see page 10), it resembles a praline, and that is why it is so delicately decorated. It may take a while to duplicate exactly how the cookie looks in the photograph, but this elegant cookie is always a huge success once people taste them. This cookie is not overly sweet, but is perfect for chocolate lovers. For this recipe you will need one round cookie cutter that is about 1½ inches (4 cm) in diameter.

MAKES ABOUT 2 DOZEN COOKIES

COOKIE DOUGH
1⅔ CUPS (200 GRAMS) ALL-PURPOSE FLOUR
⅔ CUP (75 GRAMS) CORNSTARCH
½ CUP (50 GRAMS) GROUND ALMONDS
1 CUP (100 GRAMS) CONFECTIONERS' SUGAR
1 MEDIUM EGG
2 STICKS (200 GRAMS) UNSALTED BUTTER, AT ROOM TEMPERATURE

FILLING
¾ CUP (100 GRAMS) SEMISWEET CHOCOLATE CHIPS
3½ OUNCES (100 GRAMS) MARZIPAN
1 STICK (113 GRAMS) UNSALTED BUTTER, AT ROOM TEMPERATURE

DECORATION
¾ CUP (100 GRAMS) SEMISWEET CHOCOLATE CHIPS
¾ CUP (100 GRAMS) WHITE CHOCOLATE CHIPS

1. **FOR THE COOKIE DOUGH:** Combine the dough ingredients in a bowl and, using the dough hook attachment of an electric mixer, knead until the dough is smooth, 3 to 5 minutes. Form the dough into a small loaf. Wrap the loaf in plastic wrap and let it rest in the refrigerator for about 60 minutes.

2. Preheat the oven to 400°F (200°C).

3. Lightly flour a working surface and roll the dough out thinly, about ⅛ inch (3 mm) thick. Using the round cookie cutter cut the dough into 48 circles.

4. Line a baking sheet with parchment paper and then transfer the cookies carefully to the sheet with a pastry spatula. Bake the cookies for 10 minutes until lightly golden. Be sure to not let them turn brown. Carefully remove them from the baking sheet with the pastry spatula and place them on a cooling rack to cool completely.

5. **FOR THE FILLING:** Melt the chocolate for the filling (see page 10). Grate the marzipan into a small bowl, add the melted chocolate and the butter, and mix with a fork until well combined. Scoop the filling into a paper cone (page 12) or use a teaspoon to spread 1 to 2 tablespoons of filling on half of the cookies. Top with the remaining cookies.

6. **FOR THE DECORATION:** Lightly oil a cooling rack and set aside. Melt the semisweet and white chocolates separately. Pour the melted semisweet chocolate into a small bowl and scoop the white chocolate into a paper cone. Dip one-half of the filled cookies into the bowl of semisweet chocolate and carefully place them on the oiled cooling rack.

7. Cut off just the tip of the paper cone and pipe three or four fine white chocolate lines on the dark chocolate. Using a toothpick, drag the white chocolate lines from the edge of the cookie to the center (as seen in the photograph). The decoration should resemble rows of chair backs. These cookies are good for about two weeks stored in an airtight container at room temperature.

BAKING TIP: Decorate one cookie at a time, as the dark chocolate dries quickly. If the white chocolate in the cone hardens, place it in the microwave for 10 seconds. After microwaving, test the cone with your finger to make sure the chocolate is a soft consistency.

Chocolate Mousse Cookies

Mousse is a French word that means "lather" or "foam." It is also the name of a dessert that incorporates air bubbles in cream and eggs, giving it a feathery light and airy texture. This recipe was born because I wanted to bake a chocolate mousse cake for my sister's birthday. She likes desserts, but only small quantities that are not overwhelmingly sweet. Even the most petite slice of a cake would be too much for her. This dessert is one of my lighter chocolate creations. Its fluffy texture and semisweet taste made a believer out of my sister and all of my friends, and that is why I want to share this recipe with you. For this recipe you will need one round cookie cutter that is about 1½ inches (4 cm) in diameter.

MAKES ABOUT 2 DOZEN COOKIES

COOKIE DOUGH
1¼ CUPS (160 GRAMS) ALL-PURPOSE FLOUR

1 STICK (113 GRAMS) UNSALTED BUTTER, AT ROOM TEMPERATURE

½ CUP (50 GRAMS) CONFECTIONERS' SUGAR

1 MEDIUM EGG YOLK

FILLING
1 CUP (150 GRAMS) SEMISWEET CHOCOLATE CHIPS

⅔ CUP (150 MILLILITERS) HEAVY CREAM

GRATED ZEST OF ½ ORANGE

DECORATION
1¼ CUPS (200 GRAMS) SEMISWEET CHOCOLATE CHIPS

1. **FOR THE COOKIE DOUGH:** Combine the dough ingredients in a bowl and, using the dough hook attachment of an electric mixer, knead until the dough is smooth, 3 to 5 minutes. Form the dough into a small loaf. Wrap the loaf in plastic wrap and let it rest in the refrigerator for 30 to 45 minutes.

2. Preheat the oven to 350°F (175°C).

3. Lightly flour a working surface and roll the dough out thinly, about ⅛ inch (3 mm) thick. Using the round cookie cutter cut the dough into 24 circles.

4. Lightly oil a cooling rack and set it aside. Line a baking sheet with parchment paper and then transfer the cookies carefully to the sheet with a pastry spatula. Bake the cookies for 10 to 13 minutes until lightly golden. Be sure to not let them turn brown. Carefully remove them from the baking sheet with the pastry spatula and place them on a cooling rack to cool completely.

5. **FOR THE FILLING:** Melt the semisweet chocolate in a small pot on the stove (see page 10).

6. Lightly butter tartlet molds and set aside. (If using silicone molds, you don't need to butter them.) Whip the heavy cream with an electric mixer until creamy and fluffy but not too stiff. Add the melted chocolate

and the orange zest to the warm whipped cream and stir carefully with a plastic spatula until completely mixed. Immediately remove the pan from the heat.

7. Spoon the cream mixture into the prepared tartlet mold and put it in the freezer for about 1 hour. Remove the tartlet mold from the freezer, carefully remove the chocolate mousse from the molds, and place one mousse on top of each baked cookie on the cooling rack.

8. **FOR THE DECORATION:** Melt the semisweet chocolate. Using a spoon, pour the melted chocolate over the mousse-topped cookies. Let the cookies cool at room temperature until the chocolate is firm. These cookies are good for about 1 week if kept in the refrigerator.

> **BAKING TIP:** Take the cookies out of the refrigerator at least one hour before serving time. That way, the mousse melts immediately in your mouth and tastes amazing.

Florentine Peaks

This cookie's original name is Biscotti Fiorentini. *A Florentine is a round Italian biscuit that contains almonds or hazelnuts, candied fruits, honey, and cream, with a chocolate bottom. The biscuit got its name from Florence, Italy where it originated. It later became a traditional Christmas cookie in South Germany and is also popular in Austria. The size of the biscuit varies from 1 to 5 inches or even more depending on tradition. This is an altered recipe of the original cookie with a cookie dough base. For this recipe you will need one fluted round cookie cutter that is about 1½ inches (4 cm) in diameter.*

MAKES ABOUT 3 DOZEN COOKIES

COOKIE DOUGH
2 CUPS (250 GRAMS) ALL-PURPOSE FLOUR
1¼ STICKS (142 GRAMS) UNSALTED BUTTER, AT ROOM TEMPERATURE
⅔ CUP (75 GRAMS) CONFECTIONERS' SUGAR
2 MEDIUM EGG YOLKS

TOPPING
⅓ CUP (25 GRAMS) CANDIED CHERRIES
½ STICK (57 GRAMS) UNSALTED BUTTER, AT ROOM TEMPERATURE
½ CUP (100 GRAMS) GRANULATED SUGAR
2 TABLESPOONS HONEY
½ CUP (125 MILLILITERS) HEAVY CREAM
2⅔ CUPS (400 GRAMS) SLICED ALMONDS

DECORATION
½ CUP (100 GRAMS) SEMISWEET CHOCOLATE CHIPS

1. **FOR THE COOKIE DOUGH:** Combine the dough ingredients in a bowl and, using the dough hook attachment of an electric mixer, knead until the dough is smooth, 3 to 5 minutes. Form the dough into a small loaf. Wrap the loaf in plastic wrap and let it rest in the refrigerator for about 30 minutes.

2. Preheat the oven to 350°F (175°C).

3. Lightly flour a working surface and roll the dough out thinly, about ⅛ inch (3 mm) thick. Using the round cookie cutter cut the dough into about 36 circles.

4. Line a baking sheet with parchment paper and then transfer the cookies carefully to the sheet with a pastry spatula. Pre-bake the cookies for 5 minutes. Remove the baking sheet from the oven, leaving the oven on, and place the baking sheet on a trivet.

5. **FOR THE TOPPING:** Cut the cherries into tiny pieces (they are very sticky, so they can be tricky to cut). Combine the butter, sugar, and honey in a nonstick pot and cook it on the stove over medium heat,

stirring for about 3 minutes, or until the mixture is golden brown. Add the heavy cream, increase the heat to high, and boil the filling for 2 minutes. Lower the heat, add the cherries and almonds, and cook them for 3 minutes until the filling thickens. Lightly oil a cooling rack and set it aside.

6. Spoon about one teaspoon of the filling on each pre-baked cookie. Bake the cookies a second time for 7 to10 minutes or until lightly golden. Be sure to not let the cookies turn brown. Carefully remove them from the baking sheet with the pastry spatula and place them on the oiled cooling rack to cool completely.

7. **FOR THE DECORATION:** Melt the chocolate (see page 10). Using a teaspoon pour chocolate over each cookie. Let the cookies cool at room temperature until the chocolate is firm. These cookies are good for about two weeks stored in an airtight container at room temperature.

Marzipan Rolls

This cookie was originally named Saint Gallen Bieberle, after Saint Gallen, the capital of the Canton of St. Gallen in Switzerland. Now known as simply Bieberle, it is beloved all over middle Europe and also comes with a filling of hazelnuts or almonds. The first appearance of these cookies was in the fourteenth century when they appeared in Basel and Zurich in Switzerland. The word Biberle, a shortened version of Bieberzelter or Bimenzelte, comes from the Latin noun "pigmentum," which was the name for what we now call allspice. This is one of the main ingredients of the original gingerbread spice mixture (page 10), which is used in this and many other gingerbread recipes. These cookies turn out more crunchy than soft, and the naturally sweet marzipan isn't too sweet here.

MAKES ABOUT 5 DOZEN COOKIES

FILLING
10^1/$_2$ OUNCES (300 GRAMS) MARZIPAN

COOKIE DOUGH
^{1}/$_3$ CUP (125 GRAMS) HONEY

^{1}/$_3$ CUP (75 GRAMS) PACKED BROWN SUGAR

3 TABLESPOONS COOKING OIL

1^1/$_2$ CUPS (185 GRAMS) ALL-PURPOSE FLOUR

1 TEASPOON BAKING POWDER

2 TABLESPOONS GINGERBREAD SPICE MIXTURE (PAGE 15)

1 MEDIUM EGG WHITE

DECORATION
1 MEDIUM EGG YOLK

2 TEASPOONS HEAVY CREAM

1. **FOR THE FILLING:** Dust a working surface with confectioners' sugar. Cut the raw marzipan into 4 equal pieces, and use your hands to roll them into 4 "rods" about ^{1}/$_2$ inch (1 cm) in diameter and about 6 inches (15 cm) long.

2. **FOR THE COOKIE DOUGH:** Combine the honey with the brown sugar and the oil in a saucepan and heat it over medium heat, stirring constantly, until the sugar is dissolved. Let the mixture cool off for about 2 minutes and then add the flour, baking powder, and gingerbread spice mixture. Transfer the mixture to the bowl of an electric mixer and using the dough hook attachment, beat until smooth.

3. Preheat the oven to 350°F (176°C).

4. Clean off your working surface and dust it with flour. With a rolling pin, flatten out the dough to about ^{1}/$_8$ inch (3 mm) thickness. Using a sharp knife cut the dough into 4 rectangles measuring about 2^1/$_2$ x 7 inches (6 x 15 cm).

5. Whisk the egg white in a small bowl and spread it with a pastry brush on the edges of the dough rectangles. Set a marzipan roll horizontally on each rectangle and then wrap the dough around it. Cut the rods into small triangles (you should have about 60 cookies).

6. **FOR THE DECORATION:** Combine the egg yolk and heavy cream in a bowl and whisk until well combined. Use a pastry brush to spread the mixture on the cookies.

7. Line a baking sheet with parchment paper and then transfer the cookies carefully to the sheet with a pastry spatula. Bake the cookies for 20 minutes or until lightly golden. Carefully remove them from the baking sheet with the pastry spatula and place them on the oiled cooling rack to cool completely. These cookies are good for about three weeks stored in an airtight container at room temperature.

Pistachio Love

The pistachio is a small tree originally from Persia that produces tasty nuts. Fossils and carbon dating has revealed that pistachio nuts have been part of the human diet since the late Paleolithic period. Pistachio nuts are most commonly roasted and then salted as a snack. The more difficult to find unsalted nuts are used in many pastries like Baklava (a sweet Turkish pastry) and in pralines or chocolates such as Austrian Mozartkugel "Mozart Balls". This praline was created in the year 1890 and named after Wolfgang Amadeus Mozart, the famous composer. Pistachio Love is based on the ingredients of the Mozart Ball and it is simply delicious. For this recipe you will need one round cookie cutter that is about 1½ inches (4 cm) in diameter.

MAKES ABOUT 3 DOZEN COOKIES

COOKIE DOUGH
1 CUP (100 GRAMS) CONFECTIONERS' SUGAR
3 MEDIUM EGG YOLKS
2 STICKS (210 GRAMS) UNSALTED BUTTER, AT ROOM TEMPERATURE
2½ CUPS (300 GRAMS) ALL-PURPOSE FLOUR

FILLING
14 OUNCES (400 GRAMS) MARZIPAN
⅛ CUP (30 MILLILITERS) RUM (40% PROOF ALCOHOL)
½ CUP (80 GRAMS) GROUND OR 1 CUP CHOPPED PISTACHIO NUTS

DECORATION
1 CUP (150 GRAMS) SEMISWEET CHOCOLATE CHIPS

1. **FOR THE COOKIE DOUGH:** Combine the dough ingredients in a bowl and, using the dough hook attachment of an electric mixer, knead until the dough is smooth, 3 to 5 minutes. Form the dough into a small loaf. Wrap the loaf in plastic wrap and let it rest in the refrigerator for about 60 minutes.

2. **FOR THE FILLING:** Grate the marzipan in a small bowl and use a fork to stir in the rum and pistachio nuts.

3. Preheat the oven to 350°F (175°C).

4. Lightly flour a working surface and roll the dough out thinly, about ⅛ inch (3 mm) thick. Using the round cookie cutter cut the dough into about 60 circles.

5. Line a baking sheet with parchment paper and then transfer the cookies carefully to the sheet with a pastry spatula. Take a sharp knife and press the blade lightly into the cookie making four vertical and four horizontal lines to achieve a checkerboard pattern. Bake the cookies for about 15 minutes or until lightly golden. Be sure to not let them turn brown. Carefully remove them from the baking sheet with the pastry spatula and place them on the oiled cooling rack to cool completely.

6. When the cookies are cool, spread one tablespoon of filling each on half of the cookies. Top with the remaining cookies.

7. FOR THE DECORATION: Lightly oil a cooling rack and set it aside. Melt the chocolate (see page 10) and pour it into a bowl. Dip each sandwich cookie into the chocolate, turn it 90 degrees, and dip it in the chocolate again. Place the dipped cookies on the oiled cooling rack and let them dry at room temperature until the chocolate is firm. These cookies are good for about three weeks stored in an airtight container at room temperature.

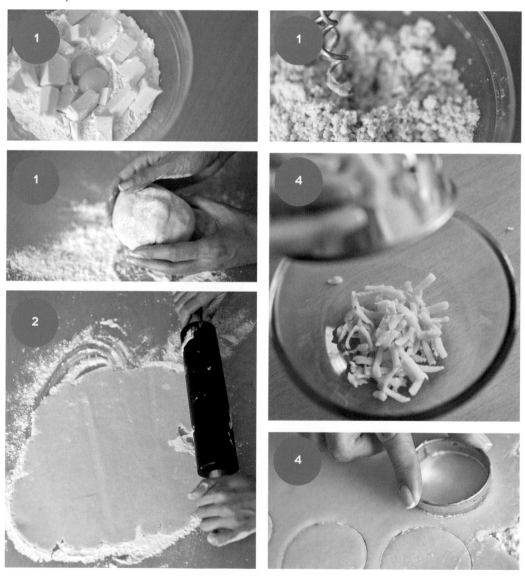

Acknowledgments

This book is the culmination of the effort of many people. I want to thank my family and close friends, you all know who you are, who believed in my dreams and pushed me directly and indirectly towards writing this book. Thank you Kristen Wiewora and Geoffrey Stone, my editors, for having faith in the project and shepherding it through the stages, to Amanda Richmond for a lovely design, and to my agent Joe Mai for making sure all the pieces came together.

Index